Surfing
the Tsunami

TODD KELSEY

DEDICATION

To my students and readers

CONTENTS

Introduction

Adapt, Adopt, Adept

(60 second summary of Introduction)

Artificial intelligence (AI) will have a significant impact on the job market, and in response I invite you to consider adopting at least one of these three perspectives:

1. Adapt (good): learn more and pay attention; keep aware of where things are headed
2. Adopt (better): adopt AI-related tools and platforms, so you can be involved in managing AI
3. Adept (best): get directly involved with developing AI, by learning coding and how to work with related data

It took almost a year for the full implications of AI to hit me. But it doesn't need to take you a year, you can just read this book. And I am not sure you can afford a year anyway - advances and announcements have been happening at an increasing pace.

One of the things that got my attention was how a small team at Google connected the Google Translate app to a deep neural network. They achieved a greater advance in six months with AI than the advances they had made in the last decade. Google was already a world leader in the accuracy of machine translation, and the results from deep learning and neural networks defied their greatest expectations. Practically speaking it was a huge advance in the accuracy of computer translation of human language, and it came from the rapidly increasing power of artificial intelligence.

In Chapter 1, *On My Radar*, I'll talk more about how artificial intelligence got on my radar and why it should get on yours, and we'll take a look at the way that artificial intelligence relates to automation.

In Chapter 2, *What is AI Up To*, we'll review the various ways that artificial intelligence has been transforming society behind the scenes, and how it is poised to come to the forefront.

I'm convinced that AI and automation will have a huge impact on the job market, and that's what motivated me to take it very seriously and write this book. In case you need convincing to take AI seriously, Chapter 3 is especially for you - I review a number of the influences, articles, studies and analysis that convinced me.

I would actually feel a sense of relief if I came across data that convinced me I could just hang loose and go back to what I was doing before, minding my own business. There are certainly people who feel like the impact will be mostly positive: they often refer to past industry transformations and imply this one will be the same, where jobs will change, and some will be lost, but others will be created. Some believe that overall *more* jobs will be created by AI than exist today, and I haven't seen evidence of this. To me the data seems to be pointing in the other direction: that there will be significant net job loss in the next 5-20 years. (But if you have any data that points to the contrary, please send it my way!)

To be clear, I am neither for nor against AI. The conversation can be polarized, with people on one side who look primarily at its benefits, and people on the other side who are alarmed at some of the potential impacts. I still remain somewhat neutral, but over the course of the last year I've been taking it increasingly seriously.

The main idea of this book has two dimensions: First, I invite you to take AI very seriously, and second, I invite you to think of your response to AI as an adventure. No matter how AI disrupts and impacts our world, I believe you can make this journey *of your own choosing*. (And if you find yourself alarmed by the data, as I did at first, I invite you to choose to live in *readiness*, not fear.)

In Chapters 4-6, I invite you to *choose* to:

- **Adapt** (good): keep an eye on things; keep yourself informed; and see what happens. You might get lucky, but you might want to review the evidence and seriously consider getting ready to . . .
- **Adopt** (better): you can adopt AI platforms and automation tools as they arise, and hopefully be the ones who manage AI and automation, until the management itself is automated; or in such a place where there is an ongoing need for human interaction. But given the fact that there don't seem to be any limits on what can be automated, it stands to reason that if AI continues to increase in sophistication; sooner or later someone will find a way to automate x, y and z; and eventually there will be a product or service

available that could replace _____. So I believe you may want to consider becoming an . . .

- **Adept** (best): yes, I am suggesting that you seriously consider becoming adept and involved in AI in some way. Maybe the data will convince you to take me seriously. Maybe if you fall into the same camp as I do, asking yourself "how could I ever do that?" . . . you might end being convinced by the data of considering another possibility: "how could I ever *not* do that?"

For what it's worth, I started my own journey simply by adapting, keeping an eye on things, and I kept thinking - "ok, maybe I can set this aside and mind my own business, and just keep doing what I was doing." But as I kept learning more, it convinced me that I needed to seriously consider being more pro-active, including exploring how to adopt AI in my field (digital marketing). Eventually as a picture formed of where things are headed and how big the disruption will be, the data convinced me to seriously consider becoming an "adept". It didn't happen overnight, but that is where I am at right now, reading books, and just about to register for a programming course, something I wouldn't have considered a year ago.

My journey took a year, but your journey might take as little as the time it takes to read this book, and some additional articles and books. And I'm saying, take AI seriously, *now*. Look at the data, especially in Chapter 3, read through chapters 4 through 6, and start at the "adapt" stage, by developing the habits of keeping an eye on things, looking at news sources, reading a book or two to get better acquainted.

Then, as soon as you're ready, I strongly recommend joining me in exploring things more closely, and seeing how you can become more adept in AI. No matter what your background is, you can do it. And I believe you *should* do it. In Chapter 7, we look closer at people and perspectives in AI - what is driving artificial intelligence, including deep learning, neural networks, the field of data science, and machine learning.

And then in Chapter 8, I review some options for next steps: books to read, courses you can take (including free online courses), and some suggestions on where you can plug-in, based on what you know right now.

(Update: Appendix A has the data I assembled and some insights from 2019; but I'd recommend taking a pass through the book as it is written first, then try taking a look at Appendix A to see if any of the insights and new links and thoughts are relevant)

Ok, so are you ready to start?

Ok, go!

No Alpha Go, that is.

-Todd

P.S. Alpha Go represents the convergence of the ancient game of Go, and a significant advance in AI, which gained a lot of attention, especially in China. To learn more about it, try searching "alpha go" on http://www.wikipedia.org

Chapter 1: Why AI - Why AI is On My Radar, Why it Should Be On Yours

In the introduction I mentioned a few things that led me to taking AI seriously, and in this chapter, I'll discuss why I came to care about the topic, how I believe it will impact you, and some background about what artificial intelligence is, including the related topic of automation.

Why I Care

In my own career, I got a traditional four year college degree, and though I grew up using computers, I mostly played games on them. I majored in Literature, and because of my interest in writing and publishing, and the educational background in my family, I started thinking about getting a Masters Degree in Communication. Then everything got sidetracked when I joined the world of rock n roll, and for awhile, this was my home:

I loved being in the studio, being onstage, being on the road, every minute of it. I was living my dream, the music was good, we had fans, but ultimately, there wasn't a hit radio single.

So then I came back to earth, and this became my home:

It was quite a shock to go from rock n roll into working in cubicles, but I learned a lot from working at my first Internet startup, and one of the most significant lessons was that things change constantly, and you can't really take anything for granted, including continued employment.

My employment went up and down, I rode waves of companies doing well, and having layoffs, and then at one point, a mentor said something very valuable to me.

They said, "Todd, you need to follow the money trail".

And all they meant by this is that it is important to understand how businesses work, and that ultimately the way a business makes money, and the departments that make money, are important. The job roles that contribute to a greater or lesser extent are important. And at the end of the day, data is important.

Data and ROI

To me, fresh-faced from the world of rock n roll, data was the last thing on my mind, but I gradually gained a great respect for it; especially the way that data relates to return on investment, or ROI.

Any business typically has investors, and the most important thing to investors is that they see a *return*. That means that the business is profitable. Business basics came slow to me but then as I worked at different companies I began to have a better understanding, including realizing that the better data that a business has, the more profitable you can be, when you are armed with the power that comes from data.

And data is something that you can act on, even as an individual. For example, one of the reasons I ended up pursuing digital marketing is because of some data that I pulled up in a free tool called Google Trends. During the middle of the Great Recession in 2009, this diagram from Google Trends showed me where Facebook was going:

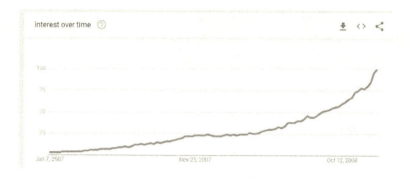

During the middle of the Great Recession, as the world economy was sliding into the abyss, I realized that digital marketing was not sliding into the abyss, and that some companies, like Facebook, were experiencing rapid growth. So I worked hard on looking at what kind of background that I had that related to digital marketing, and I sought out opportunities to learn more. It wasn't easy, and I am not some kind of startup millionaire, but I am glad that I took the opportunity to evolve. I came to learn the lesson of adapting to the times, and that is part of the reason I mention this to you.

Flash forward ten years, and Facebook is now public, has a billion members around the world, and tremendous power, primarily because of the data they have. And they, like Google and Amazon, are powerful companies that are very, very interested in the potential of artificial intelligence.

For fun, I invite you to try out Google Trends (http://trends.google.com), and type in one or two terms like "artificial intelligence" or " machine learning", and use one of the presets to look at the past year, and see where things are going. Chances are it will look something like this:

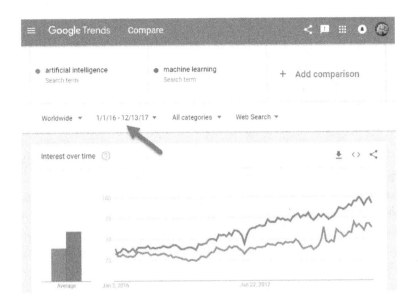

Why You Should Care

This entire book is about why you should care about AI, and what you can do about it, but the bottom line is that artificial intelligence is already having a profound impact on business, and because of the nature of technology, rapid advances are being made all the time. You may have noticed things like self-driving cars getting in the news, or how popular Amazon has become; there's a lot going on behind the scenes, and in a nutshell, artificial intelligence is helping companies all over the world to make better sense of all the increasing amounts of data that is out there.

All of these things are affecting our lives, which we'll learn more about in Chapter 2, but I'd say one of the important dimensions of AI is the way that it affects the job market, and all the data I'm seeing points to a huge impact. It will changes jobs, and take away some, and create new ones. The perspectives differ on how many jobs it will impact, and how soon it will happen, but no one can really say when, because advances in AI are *not predictable*.

If you'd like check out this related article that I wrote about three months into my journey, which I happened to publish on Linkedin on April Fool's Day. But it was no joke.

https://www.linkedin.com/pulse/dont-delay-one-can-say-how-soon-ai-take-away-jobs-todd-kelsey/
or: https://tinyurl.com/ai-jobimpact

Artificial Intelligence and Automation

It's probably safe to say that the field of artificial intelligence is in its early stages; ultimately the goal of artificial intelligence is to explore how far computers can be taken to simulate human intelligence, or potentially to exceed human intelligence. We're not there yet, but what has happened in the last few years is that significant advances have been made in artificial intelligence with respects to automation, that is, automating routine tasks. It's opened up new doors, where analyzing some kinds of complex data was previously nearly impossible, yet some parts of the analysis were repeatable and routine, and thanks to artificial intelligence and automation, are now possible.

We'll look more closely at what AI is up to these days in chapter 2, but for now I just wanted to focus on the concept of automation.

Automation: Physical Robots and Software Bots

Artificial intelligence and automation and robots are all connected. The main focus of this book is on the impact of automation through software, which is sometimes referred to as a software "bot". But in order to understand the relevance and impact, it can be helpful to think of physical robots.

Think of artificial intelligence as the brain behind either hardware or software.

Hardware Robots – autonomy and automation

When it comes to physical robot, you might have some kind of picture in your mind of what they look like. It might be something like this:

I'm not entirely sure what this robot is doing – maybe it represents taking care of pets, helping with cooking, and I don't know what's going on with its right foot. Maybe – mopping the floor with its foot?

Or your mental robot image might be something like this:

In cartoons especially, robots have sometimes been portrayed as slightly goofy, clunky, and not quite there yet, in terms of approaching "humanoid" status. In science fiction and in movies like the Terminator series, it's gone quite further than that. But in terms of the way robots result in automation, it's been mostly in terms of how they have been deployed in factories. The key thing is that most robots are not *autonomous*, yet.

For example, this diagram shows some automation in a beverage factory. This scenario involves the process of bottling, labeling and corking being automated without robots – an assembly line.

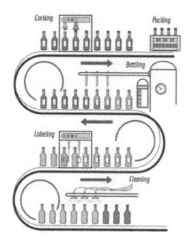

This kind of advance in physical manufacturing allowed a great many more products to be manufactured at a much higher rate. There has been a great deal of sophistication in the rise of automated manufacturing, but the entry of robots allowed things to become even more sophisticated.

For example, in automotive manufacturing, robots have been developed to assist with various facets of the manufacturing process, in some cases being faster, more efficient, and more accurate than humans, and potentially more safe.

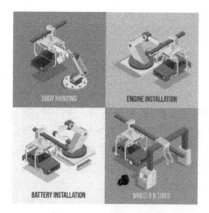

And when you connect a bunch of robots to a manufacturing process, you can have a high degree of automation and very advanced manufacturing.

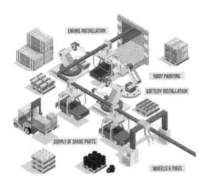

One of the questions that economists explore is the impact of automation on manufacturing. When it started to happen, many people were understandably against it. Others were for it. When you look back on it, there are differing viewpoints on whether the overall impact was to create more jobs than ones that went away, or the opposite. Regardless of the viewpoint, *highly*-automated manufacturing and *completely* automated manufacturing are here to stay.

There has been some artificial intelligence behind manufacturing robots, and the recent advances have definitely had an impact on physical manufacturing, but artificial intelligence has also had a striking impact very recently on the rise of *autonomous* robots, i.e. ones that can move around on their own.

There is a great degree of complexity in trying to get a robot to move around, even just on a flat surface, much less on uneven or unpredictable terrain. But advances in hardware and software, and artificial intelligence, have given rise recently to some robots with astonishing capabilities. Science fiction is becoming fact.

Meet the robot lineup from Boston Dynamics

By science fiction movie standards, they aren't super-realistic. But the astonishing thing is what they are starting to be able to do for the first time, with the help of artificial intelligence to help the computer processors analyze all the complex data going back and forth.

If you don't take artificial intelligence seriously, then you may at least take robots seriously after watching either of these videos. The first video was released in early 2016 and has had about 26,571,557 views at the time of writing. Atlas does some pretty advanced things for a "real" robot, due to recent advances in AI.

Boston Dynamics – Meet Atlas
https://www.youtube.com/watch?v=rVlhMGQgDkY or
https://tinyurl.com/stt-atlas

The next video was released in 2017 and shows Atlas actually doing backflips, which is incredibly difficult to program, given all the technical hurdles.

Boston Dynamics – What's New, Atlas?
https://www.youtube.com/watch?v=fRj34o4hN4I or
https://tinyurl.com/stt-atlasflips

And it's not all fun and games. People will sometimes joke about the movie series Terminator, and most experts agree we are no where near it – but we are not that far away. Some experiments are more public than others, and in 2017 Russia made some experiments public with a robot named FEDOR.

The news was released in a tweet by a Russian official. Notice the reference to algorithms.

"Robot FEDOR showed the ability to shoot from both hands. Fine motor skills and decision-making algorithms are still being improved."

Yeah. I'm glad Mr. Rogozin is pleased with his robot. Let's hope that the decision-making algorithms of both robots and humans are improved as much as possible.

Don't blame yourself if you feel like you are dreaming. If you'd like to pinch yourself, take a look at FEDOR in action.

"This Robot Shoots Guns"
https://www.youtube.com/watch?v=HTPIED6jUdU or
https://tinyurl.com/stt-fedor

I think I prefer cartoon robots. How about you?

So now that we've taken a look at physical robots, lets get back to software robots.

AI and Software Robots – more automation

I think that the detour into physical robots was worth it, both in terms of manufacturing and autonomous robots. It can be helpful to consider something physical when you try to understand what's happening in the virtual world, that is, with software.

In basic terms, what has happened with software is that over time, software applications have been designed to help people be more productive, and to accomplish tasks that may not have even been possible before without software. For example, before computers were popular you might need to do math with a calculator, and before that, with a pencil.

In the past, you might use charts to organize and enter information.

And then software like Microsoft Excel came along and allowed you to enter data into rows and columns, and to do calculations, which greatly increased the amount you could accomplish.

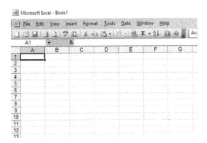

In regards to the way financial information is handled, a great transformation is going on right now, where increasing amounts of gathering and analyzing and visualizing data is done in an automated way.

If you think of the examples above as "data manufacturing", if you started with pencil and paper, and then started using calculators and spreadsheet programs, basically the manufacturing and distribution of data became increasingly automated. Tools arose to make your life easier. But there were still some things that only humans could do.

And now, with software automation, that question of what things "only a human can do" is increasingly in flux. The boundaries are being tested, just like with physical robots, and the bottom line is that you can't take anything for granted.

For awhile, software has been increasing in sophistication, and basically just taking routine tasks and automating them. But now what is happening is that even more sophisticated tasks such as the analysis of data, can and are being done with software.

It's now to the extent that you have companies like WorkFusion arising, and WorkFusion uses a term called RPA, or Robotic Process Automation. So the key thing to realize is that AI-enabled software is allowing not just the automation of tasks, but of entire *processes*.

And as we'll see more clearly in Chapter 3 (If You Need Convincing), there are significant advances happening with software automation that point to a future where increasing amounts of tasks and processes will be automated. The question is not really if, but when. And this means that it will impact the job market.

Automation, AI and Machine Learning

Before we head to the next chapter, I want to briefly mention how machine learning fits in to all that we've been discussing. Machine learning is basically the software that is currently enabling most if not all of the advances in the automation of software, and processes. To be clear, artificial intelligence and machine learning are used to control both hardware (ex: robots), and software. But the focus of this book is more on the software side.

The way to think of machine learning is probably in terms of sophistication. In science fiction, robots are sometimes indistinguishable from humans, because of their software. At this stage, while scientists and researchers are doing everything they can to increase the sophistication of artificial intelligence, in some ways it is still relatively straightforward, and mostly amounts to automation – that is, automating complex tasks and processing complex data, but the result has so far not been as complex and sophisticated as the human mind.

Basically, machine learning is an advanced way to analyze data, and recently, it has taken a turn that has allowed it to analyze information a bit more like the way the human mind analyzes data. We'll look more closely at that, but the main thing I wanted to say is that machine learning is just that: a machine learning something.

And what you have, as a result of machine learning, is the rise of things like autonomous self-driving vehicles, more advanced robots, and significant advances in "software bots", which can help to automate not only tasks, but also business processes.

Conclusion

The theme of this chapter is to discuss why you should care about AI, and the main point is that you should care, because of the increasing power of artificial intelligence, especially in the way that it is increasing automation. AI has already impacted the world in huge ways, and is poised to increase in impact. Hopefully, for the better, but I don't think we can take that for granted.

Chapter 2: What is AI Up To These Days?

In order to understand artificial intelligence, and how it's being applied these days, we're going to look at some things that may be familiar to you, both the surface, and then some of what's going on behind the scenes.

In this chapter we're going to focus on the Four A's: Autos, Advice, Automation and Analysis.

AI and Autos and Autonomy

AI and autos and autonomy, oh my! Self-driving cars and all kinds of drones are getting increasing attention these days, and advances are happening all the time, like the first cities to allow self-driving cars out on the road.

Self Driving Cars

Self-driving cars are a good example of a "visible" application of artificial intelligence, which is having a huge impact on a traditional industry: automobiles.

You can think of the concept of a self-driving car, as if a robot was driving the car, and you were the passenger.

Someday, perhaps robots will drive their own cars:

But there's a long way to go before that can happen. It's actually common to hear that phrase sometimes when people are talking about artificial intelligence. "There's a long way to go" before x, y or z is possible to do with artificial intelligence. Part of the theme of this book is to explore it, and also to keep in mind that no one really knows how far away the advances are. They could come soon, or much later.

It's all a matter of complexity, and people working to help artificial intelligence to figure out the complexity, and figure out ways of making the goal happen. A general pattern has formed where for many years, it was impossible to do _____, because of limitations in either hardware (chips, the computer), or software (the programs that run on the computer, the code).

But what's been happening in the last few years especially, is that significant advances have been happening in machine learning. That's an important phrase. Remember machine learning?

Basically machine learning involves teaching a computer how to do something. To get a bit more specific, you end up teaching a machine learning *algorithm*. The algorithm is like a hand-held calculator. It *is* a calculator, but far more advanced: it can take a great amount of data, analyze it, and provide answers. And these days, they've figured out how to use machine learning in new ways, as we'll look at later in the chapter, by making algorithms that attempt to imitate the way human brains work.

One of the areas there's been significant advances in is self-driving cars. How do you teach a car to drive? How can it possibly analyze and process all the various kinds of information around it, and how can it make good decisions?

That's a pretty complex set of problems, and the stakes are very high, in terms of safety. But in some ways, a big part of the challenge comes down to vision: taking a series of moving pictures and then analyzing them. That's a lot of data – and that's where machine learning has come in, as a tool in developing methods to help take that data, analyze it, and make decisions about what should happen next. Kind of like the human brain does, when a human is driving the car.

Google is one of the many companies working on this issue. For a number of years they've had cars driving around, with humans at the wheel, just taking pictures:

Part of the reason for this is for Google Maps, so that when you look up a location on Google Maps, in some parts of the world, you may be able to see an actual picture of the location.

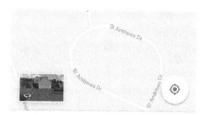

And if you click on that picture, you might see a decent picture of what is at a particular address, because of all those cars driving around with humans at the wheel.

If you want to try it out, try going to Google Maps on a desktop or laptop computer, or download the Google Maps app for iPhone or Android operating systems. Another really interesting app that comes from all of that data, is Google Street View, where not only can you see a picture, but you can explore a location, including everyday neighborhoods, cities, and historical places.

At some point Google started exploring how to use artificial intelligence to help process all of those images, and then started experimenting with allowing artificial intelligence to help drive a car, still with a human at the wheel, and at first, under carefully controlled conditions, and then out in everyday street conditions.

The Google/Waymo car is pretty small, but big enough for someone to be inside it, to watch things carefully, and gradually, as the system was developed, the machine learning process helped to analyze the data, including learning from situations where the computer made mistakes. Kind of like a human makes mistakes. Part of the point of using machine learning to train a computer, is to make educated guesses, see how things go, and improve things over time. That's exactly what Google and all the other companies and researchers are doing.

There are a lot of sensors on self-driving cars, looking every possible direction.

This results in a great deal of data, and the self-driving car has to process it and send signals back and forth, and help someone to get from point A to point B. At the time of writing, self-driving cars are not widely used, and in most places there always has to be a driver at the wheel. Companies like Google have been rightly reluctant to test "full self-driving" capability, for good reason.

As for me, I continue to be concerned about self-driving cars being let loose on the road. But in the end, I think there's a real possibility that autonomous vehicles will help more than they will hurt, and prevent more fatalities than they cause (protecting those who make the mistake of texting while driving, or driving while intoxicated).

As self-driving systems have improved, the mistakes have been reduced, and at one point a blind man convinced Google to start testing fully autonomous self-driving capability.

The blind man that convinced Google to launch a self driving car

http://www.dailymail.co.uk/sciencetech/article-4030590/The-blind-man-convinced-Google-launch-self-driving-car-firm-Steve-Mahan-revealed-person-ride-without-Google-engineer-board-says-like-driving-good-driver.html
or https://tinyurl.com/stt-steve

If you'd like to meet Steve, check out this YouTube video. It's pretty fascinating.

https://www.youtube.com/watch?v=X_d3MCkIvg8
or https://tinyurl.com/stt-steve-vid

Hardware and Software: Chips and Dip

In order to understand how artificial intelligence is helping to do things like drive cars, it's important to understand the way that hardware and software work together. You can't really have one without the other; both are important. I think hardware and software are a bit like the food item, chips and dip.

You might have a chip made out of corn that's harder, and a dip that is much softer with sour cream or just about anything, really.

Likewise, in the heart of any computer or electronic devices, there are chips made out of silicon.

The chips are all connected, and they do the heavy lifting. They have electricity running through them, and they do a lot of calculations. But chips, and circuits and all of the "hard" stuff in a computer would be worthless without software. Software is what brings a computer into action. Electricity flows through the computer, and it does something that is a little bit like thinking. It processes information, and it follows instructions. Software is like a screenplay for a computer, directing it to do things.

In the old days, software was loaded onto a computer with floppy discs, or CDs.

Nowadays, software is loaded generally from the Internet, or a device, or computer, or self-driving car, may come with software already on it.

And you can change hardware on a computer, but you're not likely to do it as often. You might add a device, upgrade the memory, remove something. But software changes all the time, it's more dynamic. A lot of things are going on, and sometimes, computers are constantly learning. The instructions that computers follow are constantly evolving, and when you look at the details, it all comes down to data, represented by 0's and 1's.

Computers are quite an amazing ecosystem. Already, most cars have some kind of computer on them, and artificial intelligence is using advanced computers in cars and help them function a bit more like a human brain.

Current generation cars are already starting to give advice, such as beeping when certain things happen, like a door is left open, or if something is wrong, even if it can't tell you. So if you keep in mind the thinking that computers are doing is not as advanced as humans, it's ok to call it thinking, or processing. And all of that processing is happening on chips.

27

The main thing to recognize is that software running on hardware, can do amazingly complex things, like drive a car.

A Closer Look at Software

You can think of running software on a computer like a treasure hunt. In machine learning, what we're trying to do is often to find answers. To get those answers, you can think of journey kind of like a hunt for treasure.

If you look at a circuit board, which is a platform for all electronics, there are a lot of paths on it.

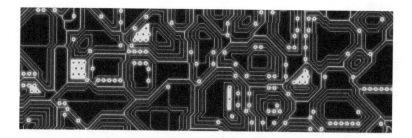

Electricity and information are travelling back and forth between a lot of different components. A circuit board can often be seen by the human eye, especially if the device you're look at is a bit older. On circuit boards, or on chips, you don't end up trying to get to a particular place on the chip –

electricity and information is just constantly moving around, kind of like a city. But when it comes on deciding what to do next, the decision-making process that a computer makes, and the software that it uses to make decisions can be thought of like as a kind of map.

A map helps you to get from point A to point B, and can help you to find things. A data map can help you to do the same thing. In the case of a self-driving car or other advanced applications of artificial intelligence, the information flow and decision-making process may form a very complex map indeed.

But the interesting thing is that in some respects, a large part of the challenge and problem-solving can be simplified and described with math. Math is at the core of artificial intelligence and machine learning. Some of the basic functions in machine learning can be represented with a pencil and a piece of graph paper.

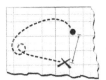

Math can be thought of a toolset, and if machine learning is a treasure hunt, math can come in very handy.

A Key to Unlock Things: If you are trying to understand where there's a pattern in some information you have, then *statistics* is a key you can use to unlock that data.

A Compass to Show Where You're Pointed: if you are trying to understand what direction your data is telling you to go, *algebra* is like a compass, than can help you figure out your direction, with angles, and when you get moving, your trajectory.

A Telescope to Find Your Goal: when you're looking for treasure in your data, to reach a certain goal, *probability* can be like a telescope, as you search for a destination that might contain what you're looking for.

If it works for you, think about machine learning and goals you can reach for as an adventure.

Drones

Drones are another very visible area where artificial intelligence is making an increasing difference.

Just the electronics alone in drones are getting more advanced all the time, giving them the ability to do a great variety of things, including flying, taking pictures and video, and looking down at the earth from up above.

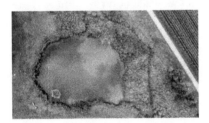

Most drones today can be controlled with a simply hand control, and like cars, have a human pilot.

That's for the kind of drone that you watch with your eyes. Keep it in sight!

But with advances in processing power and electronics, there are also increasing numbers of drones that are First Person View, or FPV, where you can look on a computer with a headset, and see what a drone is seeing.

This allows an operator to control a drone from much further away.

And now, just like artificial intelligence is allowing more autonomy in cars, self-flying capability is being built into drones as well. You can think of it a bit like if the robot were flying the vehicle.

So a drone, could be flying on its own . . .

. . . and it maybe it will use AI to stay out of the no drone zone

And as the capabilities increase, you may end up with *swarms* of drones.

We've looked at some interesting examples of ways that artificial intelligence is impacting the world of transportation and motion, with cars and drones. Now let's look at another of the four "A's": advice.

AI and Advice

Artificial intelligence is already behind a lot of things, part of the software that can impact anything from shopping to other kinds of information searching.

Siri

You may have heard about Siri – contrary to popular belief, Siri is not a digital assistant, it's actually a crab.

Siri likes the ocean, and long walks on the beach.

Ok, just kidding, Siri is a crab, but it's also an example of a number of digital assistants, which are features on many smart phones, where you can ask for information with your voice.

Processing voice is very, very complex, kind of like processing visual information for autonomous vehicles. Companies like Apple and Google have made significant advances before the onset of machine learning, but machine learning has had a remarkable impact on the accuracy of voice recognition.

While Siri and other voice-based digital assistants are nowhere near perfect, they are getting better all the time, and many people use them on a daily basis.

If you say "Siri", or "Google" to your phone, you are basically talking with your computer. Software is running on your phone, but chances are that it's also communicating to the "cloud", where a given company has a datacenter that has a lot of data. The data involved in things like voice recognition may be in a database on a computer, but it may also be increasingly burned on a chip.

For shopping in particular, there have also been an increasing number of "smart speakers", or "home assistants", who you can speak to and ask questions, order products, or if you connect them to your home, ask them to turn the lights on, etc.

Suffice to say, when all this advice is being asked for, it's a lot of data that you're talking about, and machine learning, which is part of artificial intelligence, is doing a lot of the heavy lifting. Siri and Alexa and Google and others make mistakes all the time, but the point is, they're learning, and they're getting better.

AI and Automation – Physical and Virtual

One of the central powers of artificial intelligence, when coupled with the right software and hardware, is the ability to automate things, and as you'll see throughout this book, the advances in AI indicate that just about anything can be automated, sooner or later. The most visible forms of automation have been occurring in the visible world.

Physical Process

Automation generally involves a process, some kind of routine action that a smart enough robot can duplicate. Robots have been in factories for some time, and their capabilities were increasing long before the current explosion of artificial intelligence. Over time, more complex tasks became possible with better programming, but the tasks were still fairly routine, even if they were complex, and a good example is in manufacturing.

As we saw in the first chapter, robots are used in a variety of tasks in manufacturing.

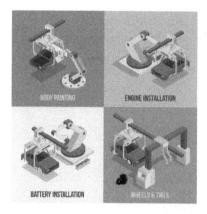

And when you put all those tasks together, it becomes a process.

Manufacturing is a good example of a physical process, and it relies heavily on hardware, especially the chips that go inside computers.

Virtual Process

The newest thing that is happening with artificial intelligence, which is poised to have a significant impact on the job market, is the automation of virtual processes. That is, when tasks are partly, mostly, or totally digital, it is increasingly possible to automate them. Digital = virtual.

For example, an accountant might use a spreadsheet program, and enter and manipulate data.

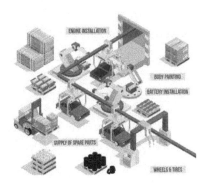

The spreadsheet program is like a tool, which an accountant can use to speed up a process. And long before artificial intelligence, spreadsheet programs had a number of features to help speed up routine tasks. There are a number of business processes that have largely been managed within spreadsheet programs.

If you think of data like a product, data management is like a manufacturing process, within a factory.

When you're talking about the complexity of data processing, it's good to think in terms of paths. A manufacturing plant has an assembly line, where there's generally a single or primary path. As the item goes through manufacturing, such as a car, various pieces are added, and you end up with a finished product. Similarly, you might have a data project in a spreadsheet program, and you might follow a fairly straightforward process to arrive at the report.

But in business as in manufacturing, the larger the scale, the larger the complexity. And the path that products or data takes can get significantly more complex. The product might take one general path through a factory, but then you have to consider the path that the product takes to get to the customer, as well as the path that ingredients and parts take, to get to the product.

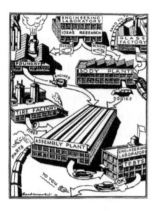

For some reason, this kind of process reminds me of board games. Maybe I'm just trying to think of a way to make it fun. But there's a decent, familiar parallel, if you've ever played a board game, and it relates directly to some of the basic concepts in machine learning, and automating processes. In a typical board game, you might roll the dice, and move in a fairly predictable path around the board.

In other games, you follow a path that curves a bit, but in some cases, you can jump ahead.

And in some games, the paths that you can follow area a lot more complex. You end up with a lot more options, which involve probability (rolling the dice), and decision-making (choosing where to move your piece).

This process of decision-making in board games reminds me of a fundamental blueprint in data processing and machine learning. A board game can be like a flowchart in some ways.

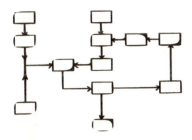

A flowchart is basically the simplest visual way to represent a path you can take, with a variety of options. It's often used in business to represent processes, such as decision-making processes. If the budget is sufficient, move on to research on purchasing equipment. Is the price good enough? Yes or No. And so on.

Since many of these processes in business are increasingly *virtual*, that is, made with the aid of digital tools, it becomes easier to automate the processes. The more routine they are, the easier it is to automate the virtual process. And as we'll see in the next section, even analysis can be automated and performed by machine learning.

For the office worker, this is likely to bring significant changes.

It is entirely possible that some processes will be entirely automated. There has been a conversation going on about just how much can be automated, and when. Some say that it will happen sooner than later, and are very concerned. Both sides agree that it is possible that some jobs may go away, where humans will be replaced with algorithms, which are essentially like robots.

The disagreement is mainly about how much can be automated, and how soon. And optimists generally feel that when you look at past transformations, where technology impacts society, people initially feared that there would be mass unemployment, and then eventually, more jobs were created, as a result of the demand for new products and services. The optimist view is that for society, for the large part, artificial intelligence will lead to a large number of life changing discoveries and tools, which will help us to be safer, and more productive:

But no matter what side of the spectrum people are on, most experts agree that it's important to take artificial intelligence very seriously, and that's the goal of this book, is to help you to learn about it, and convince you to pay attention.

But when and if you are convinced, I also think that having fun is a great way to help with the learning process, and I think it's fair to think about the way automation works as a game, including business process.

AI and Analysis

Analysis is the most sophisticated form of artificial intelligence, and in some ways, it happens at every level – when you are talking about a car or drone, there's lots of analysis going on, about what to do next. When you are offering advice to the home shopper, identifying someone's speech, or automating a process, likewise.
In some ways, analyzing data, and delivering analysis to people, is like a process. Just a lot more complex, sometimes infinitely so.

When it gets down to the way machine learning works, if you reduce it down to it's most basic form, it still comes down to something like a flowchart.

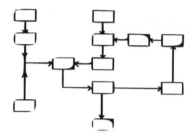

And ultimately, hopefully the analysis will help you to make a decision. It may be analysis that helps you decide which option to take, which way to go.

The analysis and recommendations may also be like a maze, where several paths can be followed. At any given point in the journey, you might choose to go in multiple directions. Those choices have consequences, and you are probably working towards a goal.

In some ways, the process of human thought can be thought of as a maze. Information flows through the brain, you have experiences, some of the information is stored or remembered, other information is forgotten. Sometimes you are working on approaching a goal, and there are multiple ways to get there. Sometimes you have to make a decision.

Sometimes, thinking is like going through a maze.

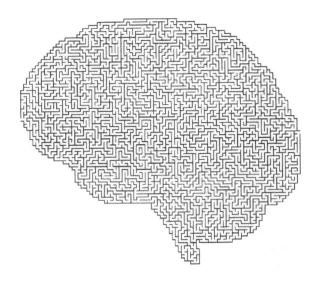

A Maze of Neurons: Machine Learning and Neural Networks

We're just going to scratch the surface here, but it's important to note that some of the most striking advances in artificial intelligence have come from looking at the way our brains work. And when you get down to the most basic part of the brain, you end up with a neuron.

Hi neuron.

Neurons are a building block in the brain, and when you connect them together, it looks a bit like this next image:

Or this:

Does this last image remind you of anything? To me it looks like a tree, and it looks like neurons. I think that's because sometimes in nature there are universal patterns. In this case, it's because neurons are dynamic; they grow.

Neurons form, and grow

In the present generation of chips, the pathways etched in silicon are mostly fixed. The information and electricity that flow through them are dynamic, and software itself is very dynamic, but the paths themselves are relatively fixed. In a new generation of chips being developed, called neuromorphic chips, there is some movement towards a chip that can grow and adapt in certain ways (morph = change). But at the present time, the chips themselves are fixed – the hardware, is fixed.

But they started experimenting with simulating a network of neurons, in software. In the human brain neurons do form a network, and help you make decisions. In artificial intelligences, algorithms attempt to analyze situations based on a lot of information, and recent advances in machine learning attempt to model analysis of data on the human brain, something like the way that a network of neurons works.

So if we return to our friendly neuron, we are looking at it in an isolated state.

But when the capability of a network of neurons is applied to analysis and decision making, it is similar in one sense to a flow chart, or decision tree, where you start out with a variety of options, and attempt to narrow it down to one.

Similarly, you could represent a set of neurons connected to each other, in a similar way, which can help you understand how neural networks work.

A given set of neurons in the human brain may connect to another set, and electrical impulses can represent thought or sensory information. Electrical impulses flow, and they may just be gathering data, or going through a process of learning, where a decision is made. Options are considered, and a course of action is chosen.

When you start to learn about neural networks, it's very interesting how *importance* plays a part. Is the information or impulse important? Promote it! In a radical oversimplification, a neural network in artificial intelligence looks at a set of data, and criteria for a goal are established at the other end, which represent the ideal outcome, such as recognizing a cat. A great deal of approaches and options and calculations are made, and when something seems to work, it can be promoted to another level of the network. Gradually, the network "learns", and it can get better over time at analyzing. It's a bit like the diagrams above.

Even though diagrams with straight lines are nice and clean, you just have to remember that in the human brain, and even in digital, neural networks, the connections are a lot more complex.

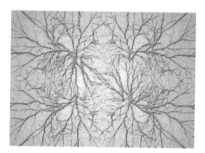

Does the network of neurons look convoluted at all? It does to me. Scientists are only beginning to just understand what the neurons are doing, but they've been able to learn enough to greatly increase the ability of computers to analyze some kinds of data. Still, it can get convoluted, and there's even a particular kind of neural network called a *convolutional* neural network.

Thankfully, researchers and companies are working on tools to reduce the complexity of using the power of artificial intelligence, even as they work on approaching more complex tasks and systems.

It's no mistake then that artificial intelligence is closely related to science. It actually *is* a science, sometimes called data science. No one that I know of calls themselves an artificial scientist, but plenty of people call themselves data scientists. Part of the point of this book is to suggest that there are many different ways to be a data scientist, but I'm firmly convinced of three things:

1) Everyone *is* already a data scientist in a sense. We use data all the time to make decisions.
2) Everyone can learn *more* about how to use data.
3) Because of where things are headed, everyone *should* consider becoming a data scientist in some capacity, with a spirit of adventure and exploration, and even fun.

AI and Science

To return to the brain, neuroscience itself is one of the primary areas related to artificial intelligence. Neuroscience is helping us understand the human brain, the way it works, and the field has a huge impact on "practical" artificial intelligence and machine learning. And in turn, machine learning has helped neuroscientists look at the data they are gathering and make better sense of it.

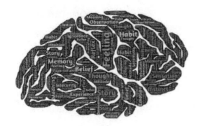

Health and Diagnosis

You can probably look at just about any field of science these days and explore how it is being impacted by machine learning. One familiar are though may be diagnosis.

Just like an ecommerce site like Amazon may give you advice, medical professionals also give advice, after analyzing your condition. In many cases this involves diagnosis. They look at your symptoms, they may consult some references, but they also have experience, and intelligence, and can often come up with a good diagnosis of what the issue is.

There's a lot of data in medical databases, and what's been happening is that discoveries have been made that show where machine learning has allowed researchers to look at vast databases that an individual doctor could never hope to memorize, and the algorithm can actually identify what's wrong. And yes, there have already been instances of algorithms that have been proven to be more accurate than doctors with diagnosis.

It doesn't mean that doctors will be replaced, per se – but most patients would probably want a more accurate diagnosis, and the amount of training for certain areas of medicine may decrease, as the tools themselves increase in power. Will there be a robot doctor? Maybe not anytime soon, but there are already robotic surgeries, in some cases more accurate and consistent than human-managed surgeries, and the trend is sure to continue.

Basically artificial intelligence is advancing in every area of medicine, including extremely complex situations, especially where there is a lot of data. Including genetics, for example.

If the human genome is like a puzzle, then scientists are making significant advances in being able to understand and analyze the data in DNA. (And they are starting to "program" DNA).

Space

One of my favorite areas where AI is having an impact is in looking at outer space. There's a lot of information that's fairly complex, and scientists are starting to harness AI to help solve some of the hardest mysteries, which could eventually help us understand and travel to other planets.

Astrophysicists are using AI to analyze data 10 million times faster than before

http://www.businessinsider.com/astrophysicists-neural-net-ai-analyse-gravitational-lensing-2017-8

AI *is* Science

I do think it's helpful to remember that AI is a science, and that in today's world, science has no borders. I do believe competition is good, and that it is healthy for universities, companies and countries to compete. But I also think that science has been an area where cross pollination and collaboration between scientists from different countries has made some of the greatest advances possible.

Therefore I encourage you when considering AI and learning about it, to consider what's going on in other countries. Here are a few articles I invite you to read along these lines.

Google opens Chinese AI lab, says 'science has no borders'

https://www.theverge.com/2017/12/13/16771134/google-ai-lab-china-research-center

One interesting dynamic has been the research and commitment that China has made in artificial intelligence. That has some people worried, but others believe more in collaboration than confrontation, and to a certain extent, Google is pursuing this path in China.

Interview: Google AI top scientist calls China an "important country" for AI

http://news.xinhuanet.com/english/2017-12/20/c_136839363.htm

> *"China is a rising country of AI work and research," said Fei-Fei Li, Chief Scientist of Artificial Intelligence (AI) and Machine Learning (ML) at Google Cloud, calling for enhanced AI cooperation between major countries. She acknowledged that AI is viewed by some as a new source of competition between countries. However, as a scientist, Li said she believes science has no national boundary, and she hopes to see more cooperation and communication across borders.*

I think Fei Fei Li is very interesting, and I appreciate how she has worked at Google in the United States, and is headed to help Google work with AI in China.

Perhaps this is what Fei Fei Li looked like as a child.

In my opinion, the more science, the better. May new generations arise and become scientists.

And data scientists, of course.

It's Never Too Late

One last word in this chapter, especially for anyone who is already convinced of the importance of AI, and even the importance of *learning* AI, but they feel too old for it.

The truth is, it's never to late to learn to code. Need convincing?

It's never too late to learn to code

http://kernelmag.dailydot.com/issue-sections/features-issue-sections/11472/seniors-learn-to-code-general-assembly/

Some People Learn to Code in Their 60s, 70s or 80s

https://www.nytimes.com/2017/09/22/your-money/some-people-learn-to-code-in-their-60s-70s-or-80s.html

To save the economy, teach grandma to code

https://www.pbs.org/newshour/nation/save-economy-teach-grandma-code

I think it's important to consider opposing viewpoints, and not everyone is "pro-coding":

Please don't learn to code

https://techcrunch.com/2016/05/10/please-dont-learn-to-code/

But I'd say that even in the article above, the author is not suggesting that people don't learn to code; they are just suggesting some things to keep in mind. When you read into their claims, they're not even saying that there isn't opportunity. They are just suggesting that it takes work.

Finally, this article is particularly good. I dare you to read it, no matter what age you are.

3 Myth-Busting Reasons to Start Coding Even at an Older Age

https://www.makeuseof.com/tag/3-myth-busting-reasons-start-coding-even-older-age/

AI and _____

If you haven't already guessed, every field is likely to be impacted by AI, sooner or later. Another lesson about AI is that things are in flux, and always evolving.

So part of the idea behind looking at what AI is up to these days, is an invitation to join me, in *evolving*. And the point of the previous section is to make it clear that it's never too late.

Ahoy, mateys! Get out your key, and your compass, and your telescope!

Chapter 3 - If You Need Convincing to Take Action: Consider Data on AI's Impact on the Job Market

No matter what, in all the articles I've read, from the darkest pessimism and alarm, all the way to the rosy glow of optimism about AI, no one I have read suggests that it's ok to ignore AI. In general, everyone seems to overwhelmingly agree that *no one* should be passive, and that *everyone* should take AI seriously.

As you look at what people say in news, and books and discussions, there does seem to be some polarization: there are optimists, and there are pessimists. No matter what your perspective is, I urge you to be a *realist*.

As soon as you are convinced to take AI very seriously, you can skip this chapter. The suggested definition of taking AI seriously is not only reading the rest of this book, but actually taking action based on the next 3 chapters especially. If you read this book, or part of it, and you find yourself not taking action, then it means you are not really taking AI seriously. You should probably come back and read this chapter more carefully, and more completely, and invest time and money if necessary, in reading more of the resources I point to, which convinced me to take action, to write this book for you. If you don't take action, it's a waste. Take action. Read the chapter and consider the data. Discuss it. Share it. Debate it. Act on the data.

There's been enough evidence that it convinced me to take action, in spite of all the other things I have going on. I can totally see most or all readers of this book being busy – but what I'm saying is that no matter how busy you are, there's enough data out there to convince me to start taking action, and I believe very strongly you should take action, immediately.

Three perspectives: Optimist, Pessimist and Realist

As you look at the data, I invite you to consider various perspectives, both of the writers, and your own. I especially invite you to consider perspectives that oppose your own. Some people fall naturally into certain categories, others don't. As for me, I want to be an optimist, the data tempts me to be a pessimist, and I'm working on becoming a realist. You might be similar or completely different.

I recommend digging. Sometimes when you dig in data, you can find treasure. When you listen to what people say or watch videos or television or read what people write, dig beneath the surface. What is the bias of the person presenting the data? Or are they just speculating or presenting their opinion? (ex: did they actually present any data to support their position).

Dig for data. Dig for treasure. Ask yourself: how deep is the data, how good is it? How complete is it? Am I willing to be challenged? Have I spent any time digging for opposing viewpoints? Am I acting on reflex, or am I really looking at what the data is saying? All good questions.

I also invite you to ask yourself some questions when you look at the idea, based on your perspective. I invite you to challenge your perspective – challenge others, challenge me. Ideally, with data.

The Optimist: Focus on the Good

If you are an AI optimist, or think you might be one, consider these questions when you look through the data.

Q1: Based on the fact that so much of work is already digital, do you think it's possible the impact of AI may be larger and more rapid than the impact from past technologies?

Q2: If so, do you think that short-term and long-term, the number of jobs AI creates could be less than the jobs AI replaces?

Q3: Would you agree that everyone should take some form of action, such as Adapting and learning more about AI, Adopting AI when possible to be actively involved, and ideally becoming Adept in AI?

The Pessimist: Act on the Real Possibility that Things Could Get Very Ugly

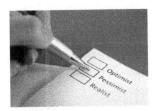

If you are a AI pessimist, or think you might be one, consider these questions when you look through the data.

Q1: Based on the data from studies such as McKinsey, do you think it's possible that AI and automation could create more jobs than they replace?

Q2: If you think there could be massive job loss and increasing economic inequality, what kind of response do you think individuals, companies or governments should support to create new jobs, such as investing in workforce redevelopment, infrastructure, or renewable energy? If you believe in resisting AI, when you look at past precedents, do you believe people could and should be protected by some form of regulation, or wealth redistribution from negative taxation or universal basic income? Do you believe such efforts are sustainable at the level of a single country, or that they require universal ratification? If you believe they require universal ratification, do you believe that it is possible or likely in an atmosphere of global competition?

Q3: Would you agree that everyone should take some form of action, such as Adapting and learning more about AI, Adopting AI when possible to be actively involved, and ideally becoming Adept in AI?

The Realist: Act on the Data, both Good and Bad

Maybe with AI, the glass is not half full, or half empty, maybe it's both. Maybe it will be in a new episode of the show Big Bang Theory. Maybe the glass can be like a wave/particle duality, or a quantum entanglement. But don't worry, you don't need to be a science geek to understand AI. (Though I'd like to tempt you into becoming one, at least secretly.)

I encourage you to become an AI realist, and consider these questions when you look through the data.

Q1: Based on the data, do you think it's possible the impact of AI may be larger and more rapid than the impact from past technologies?

Q2: Would you agree that everyone should take some form of action, such as Adapting and learning more about AI, Adopting AI when possible to be actively involved, and ideally becoming Adept in AI?

Q3: If you are convinced that you should take action, do you think it should be private, confined to your personal life, or that you should go public, and advocate for your community and country to take AI seriously?

The DATA

In this section, I list most of the articles and influences that convinced me to take AI very seriously. These links focus mainly on the impact on the job market, but in new editions and on the website, I will add links that are more general, including advances in the sophistication of AI, like the introduction of AutoML, that convinced me there was urgency to writing this book.

NOTE re: SITE – most or all of these links are available for easy clicking at http://tsunami.ai/links

NOTE re: PAID NEWS: Some of the paid news sites allow free limited access, and some have discounts for faculty and students as well. Personally, as part of arming yourself with data and to take AI more seriously, I think it's worth investing in a subscription to some or all of these news sources, and then scanning them once a week. Things change rapidly every year.

MOST RECENT

It Was a Big Year for A.I.
http://www.slate.com/blogs/future_tense/2017/12/28/year_in_artificial_i ntelligence_most_impressive_ai_and_machine_learning.html
2017 has been a booming year for the field of artificial intelligence. While A.I. and data-focused machine learning have been around for decades, the algorithmic technologies have made their presence known in a variety of industries and contexts this year.

> A good recap

Will Robots Take Our Children's Jobs?
https://www.nytimes.com/2017/12/11/style/robots-jobs-children.html?_r=0
Artificial intelligence may make half of today's jobs obsolete in 20 years. What careers

will be left when our children grow up?

Some of the World's Largest Employers No Longer Sell Things, They Rent Workers

https://www.wsj.com/articles/some-of-the-worlds-largest-employers-no-longer-sell-things-they-rent-workers-1514479580

"The large outsourcers are using a combination of analytics and automation to significantly reduce the need for labor"

> Like many articles mentioned in this chapter, this particular article could fall into several categories, but I think it highlights the dimension of how automation is already impacting jobs. It speaks to the phenomena of the gig economy, where companies are increasingly taking advantage of part-time workers to quickly scale up and scale down when needed. I think it's an important article to consider reading, along with many of the others from WSJ, and worth subscribing to for that reason (remember students/faculty can get a discount). Another category this article can fall into is international, where the phenomena of outsourcing has inadvertently resulted in some countries being more exposed to automation, such as India.

The common dynamic in the various categories, and the important thing to understand, is that work is being increasingly "disaggregated", isolated into tasks, and outsourcing in general can result in the related work being easier to automate. And this particular article is a good example that shows how the impact of AI on the job market is not just speculation, it is *happening*.

In short, when you look at the trends and phenomena represented in the articles above and throughout this chapter, I do believe it will help you to take AI more seriously, and "prioritize" it. Skimming the articles is better then not reading them, but case in point, with the article above, I think that investing the time/money in reading the articles can help make things very concrete. AI isn't theoretical or a mental exercise, or somewhere off in the future. It's having an impact right now, and the impact will continue to grow in strength. Hence the idea of surfing the tsunami. Read, learn, take it seriously. And as you see in the next chapter, make the habit of taking the time to read as many articles as you are willing to, weekly, or even daily. I guarantee it's worth it.

GOOD NEWS – LEARN FROM SWEDEN

The Robots Are Coming, and Sweden Is Fine
https://mobile.nytimes.com/2017/12/27/business/the-robots-are-coming-and-sweden-is-fine.html
In a world full of anxiety about the potential job-destroying rise of automation, Sweden is well placed to embrace technology while limiting human costs.

In a nutshell, there are plenty of opportunities to be optimistic, *if* a society invests enough in its citizens.

I think in some ways this article is one of the best I have ever read on AI and automation, because it addresses the disruption, and shows how critical safety nets are. Regardless of what someone thinks about the politics of socialism and capitalism, if you look at the stories in this article, the fact is that Sweden has safety nets in place that will greatly help its citizens to navigate disruption. I think it is critical to consider their example; yes there is economic wealth in Sweden, but it's not just a question of wealth, it's a question of what Sweden has chosen to invest in, and the citizens' willingness to accept higher taxation – in this mindset, the needs of the many outweigh the needs of the few.

As you look at the data, and see how serious the situation is worldwide, I think it's helpful to consider the example of Sweden in the back of your mind, and if you are willing to think beyond your own situation, at the very least this article highlights how important safety nets are of one kind or another. There is a lot of social inequity already, and if it isn't clear to you yet, it should be clear after reading the articles in this chapter, the social inequity is likely to get bigger, and result in accelerating the amount of suffering that is already going on. The political questions are inescapable – and if you don't want taxes to increase, what's the alternative? Maybe private safety nets, maybe universal basic income, or voluntary wealth sharing from something like www.rgbexchange.org.

No single approach would be enough, and America is unfortunately likely to resist expanding safety nets, but the longer we delay, the worse off we will be, and sooner or later there will be a backlash – but there doesn't have to be done. There are ways to help people evolve to a changing economy, and I believe there are ways to strengthen public and private safety nets. It may involve sacrifice, but if you are willing to consider the genetic fact that we are all related, I think it's fair to think of society as extended family, and I'm not so sure any individual can claim to have arrived at their wealth without the support of the society around them. From that standpoint, I believe that whatever we have to do is worth paying for.

We're talking about millions more people losing their jobs at the worst, or at the best, having to transition to new jobs – but support is needed either way – it's not going to happen magically. To face the disruption of AI as a society will require transforming parts of the society – the society has to adapt, adopt, and become adept; it's no mistake that China has declared itself as an "AI-first" country.

As for me, I think that even in America, there is already a need for stronger safety nets, and that Americans should seriously consider the highly unusual situation in Sweden in regards to automation and AI – the reason they are relatively secure heading into the disruption is because the citizens are *well-supported*.

So I invite you to not only read the article about Sweden and keep it in mind, but hold it in your mind to contrast with all the data and implications in this chapter, and consider not only taking action to become more involved in AI in your own life, but also consider advocating for your government and country to take action to help people navigate the disruption. The more passive we are as individuals and countries, the worse off we will be. And conversely, the more active we are in confronting the disruption of AI, the better off we will be. I think Sweden's approach speaks for itself, and I hope you consider reading the article.

INTERACTIVE

21 Jobs of the Future

https://www.cognizant.com/perspectives/21-jobs-of-the-future
Concern about a jobless future has never been greater. Seemingly every day, an academic, researcher or technology leader suggests that in a world of automation and artificial intelligence (AI), workers will increasingly be a surplus to what businesses need. For many people, the future of work looks like a bleak place, full of temporary jobs, minimum wage labor and a ruling technocracy safely hidden away in their gated communities.

Automation Job Impact Calculator - Will a robot take your job?
http://www.bbc.com/news/technology-34066941
Find out the likelihood that your job will become automated in the next two decades

GENERAL

Meet Your New Boss: An Algorithm
https://www.wsj.com/articles/meet-your-new-boss-an-algorithm-1512910800
Traditional employers like General Electric are using artificial intelligence and other elements of the work-on-demand business model to manage traditional full-time workforces, and automate workforce management tasks

Robots: Is your job at risk?
http://money.cnn.com/2017/09/15/technology/jobs-robots/index.html
Coaches and barbers can let out a deep breath. Drivers and fast food cooks? Not so much.

Wall Street's Endangered Species: The College Jock
https://www.wsj.com/articles/wall-streets-endangered-species-the-ivy-league-jock-1495721462
For decades, banks and brokers stocked trading floors with collegiate athletes. These days, the ex-jocks are getting sidelined by machines

IMPACT ON SPECIFIC JOB TYPES

Goodbye high seas, hello cubicle. Sailor -- the next desk job.
http://money.cnn.com/2017/05/19/technology/autonomous-ships-sailor-desk-job/index.html
Sailors, pilots and drivers shift from the high seas, blue skies and open roads as their jobs become automated.

Talk Is Cheap: Automation Takes Aim at Financial Advisers—and Their Fees
https://www.wsj.com/articles/talk-is-cheap-automation-takes-aim-at-financial-advisersand-their-fees-1501099600
Services that use algorithms to generate investment advice, deliver it online and charge low fees are pressuring the traditional advisory business

Robots Will Soon Do Your Taxes: Bye Bye Accounting Jobs
https://www.wired.com/2017/02/robots-will-soon-taxes-bye-bye-accounting-jobs/
Opinion: Between accounting professionals and truck drivers alone, about 4.5 million human jobs could be ceded to robots over the next few years.

Companies Leave Bean Counting to the Robots
https://www.wsj.com/articles/companies-leave-bean-counting-to-the-robots-1508407203
Large corporations world-wide are increasingly turning to robotic software in an effort to cut costs, liberate workers from repetitive tasks and, in many cases, reduce finance-department employee numbers.

Nokia to Automate Finance Tasks in Bid to Cut Headcount
https://blogs.wsj.com/cfo/2017/08/31/nokia-to-automate-finance-tasks-in-bid-to-cut-headcount/
Nokia Corp. is looking to automate forecasting and reporting tasks in a bid to cut the headcount of its finance function, according to finance chief Kristian Pullola.

Your Lawyer May Soon Ask This AI-Powered App for Legal Help
https://www.wired.com/2015/08/voice-powered-app-lawyers-can-ask-legal-help/
Using the same IBM tech that let a computer beat humans at Jeopardy, a new tool could put an end to legal gruntwork.

Lawyer-Bots Are Shaking Up Jobs
https://www.technologyreview.com/s/609556/lawyer-bots-are-shaking-up-jobs/
AI is augmenting and automating the tasks currently performed by hundreds of thousands of people in the U.S. alone.

AI in Law and Legal Practice – A Comprehensive View of 35 Current Applications
https://www.techemergence.com/ai-in-law-legal-practice-current-applications/
From 'automated contract analysis' to 'legal document summarization', this article breaks down 35 unique applications of AI in law and the legal profession.

How the Growth of E-Commerce Is Shifting Retail Jobs
https://www.nytimes.com/interactive/2017/07/06/business/1000000051 87607.mobile.html?_r=0
Although online shopping companies have created hundreds of thousands of jobs, they have not directly made up for the losses at traditional retailers, and the new jobs tend to be concentrated in a small number of large cities.

Microsoft to Cut Up to 4,000 Sales and Marketing Jobs
https://mobile.nytimes.com/2017/07/06/technology/microsoft-to-cut-up-to-4000-sales-and-marketing-jobs.html
"This is being done mainly to evolve the skill sets we need," said Frank Shaw, a Microsoft spokesman.

AUTOMATION AND AI

Technology Ushers In a New Distributive Economy
https://blogs.wsj.com/cio/2017/11/24/technology-ushers-in-a-new-distributive-economy/
Intelligence is no longer just housed in the brains of human workers, but emerging through the constant interactions among machines, software and processes. As machines start to exhibit associative intelligence, something we thought only humans could do, current economic rules no longer apply, writes CIO Journal Columnist Irving Wladawsky-Berger.

INSIDE ADIDAS' ROBOT-POWERED, ON-DEMAND SNEAKER FACTORY
https://www.wired.com/story/inside-speedfactory-adidas-robot-powered-sneaker-factory/
When its first stateside Speedfactory opens in Atlanta, Adidas will be chasing the future of automated manufacturing in America, too.

"The Relentless Pace of Automation"
https://www.technologyreview.com/s/603465/the-relentless-pace-of-automation/
Artificial intelligence could dramatically improve the economy and aspects of everyday life, but we need to invent ways to make sure everyone benefits.

ROBOTIC PROCESS AUTOMATION

Robotic process automation is one of the ways that tasks in some categories above will be automated. This is data about the market growth, meaning how rapidly it is being adopted.

The Robotic Process Automation market will reach $443 million this year
https://www.horsesforsources.com/RPA-marketsize-HfS_061017

RPA Market Size Projected To Reach $8.75 Billion By 2024
https://www.grandviewresearch.com/press-release/global-robotic-process-automation-rpa-market
RPA market is expected to reach USD 8.75 billion by 2024, according to a new report by Grand View Research, Inc.

ADOPT

Making Yourself Irreplaceable Before Artificial Intelligence Learns to do Your Job
https://www.entrepreneur.com/article/303457
The best way to avoid losing your job to a robot is learn how to do your job working with one.

ADAPT, EVOLVE, ADEPT

Learn a Language, but Not a Human One
https://www.wsj.com/articles/learn-a-language-but-not-a-human-one-1500229654
Fluency in coding is a more useful skill than French, Spanish or Russian.

That 'Useless' Liberal Arts Degree Has Become Tech's Hottest Ticket
https://www.forbes.com/sites/georgeanders/2015/07/29/liberal-arts-degree-tech/#19ee4e46745d
Stop thinking of Silicon Valley as an engineer's paradise. There's far more work for liberal arts majors -- who know how to sell and humanize.

> Author's Comment: there's a lot of controversy about higher education and the liberal arts these days. I believe the overall data points to there being value in a liberal arts degree – but you should also develop technical fluency, in my opinion. For example, students from Harvey Mudd are some of the most sought-out students in Silicon Valley, and their "ROI" is rated high – because they have tech skills, but also know how to *communicate*. See next article.

(report mentions Harvey Mudd)

WHY IT'S WORTH IT TO STUDY LIBERAL ARTS – EVEN IF YOU'RE GOING INTO STEM

https://www.payscale.com/career-news/2017/04/worth-study-liberal-arts-even-youre-going-stem

As more tech companies hire workers without degrees, and career changers shift to coding jobs after completing non-degree bootcamps, it's fair for the prospective college student to wonder if getting a degree is still worth it. For the time being, at least, the answer is yes — you're still a more competitive candidate with a degree than without one. College graduates on average out-earn workers with a high school diploma, who make just 62 percent of their degree-holding peers' earnings.

BE MORE HUMAN

How to Prepare for an AI Future (Hint: Be More Human)

https://www.cognizant.com/perspectives/how-to-prepare-for-an-ai-future-hint-be-more-human

The rise of artificial intelligence is the great story of our time. Decades in the making, AI-infused machines will soon change our lives and work in ways that are easy to imagine but hard to predict.

WORKERS DISPLACED BY AUTOMATION SHOULD TRY A NEW JOB: CAREGIVER

https://www.wired.com/story/workers-displaced-by-automation-should-try-a-new-job-caregiver/

Opinion: You don't want a robot taking care of your baby; the aged need to be loved, to be listened to, fed, and sung to.

REGULATE

How to Regulate Artificial Intelligence

https://mobile.nytimes.com/2017/09/01/opinion/artificial-intelligence-regulations-rules.html

Robot Tax – A Summary of Arguments "For" and "Against"
https://www.techemergence.com/robot-tax-summary-arguments/
What happens if a new technology causes millions to lose their jobs in a short period of time, what if most companies simply no longer need any human . . .

INEQUITY/GIG ECONOMY

Workplace robots could increase inequality, warns IPPR
http://www.bbc.com/news/business-42493529
The government must intervene to stop automation driving up wage inequality, a think tank has warned. The Institute for Public Policy Research said robots would not necessarily be bad for the economy. However, it warned lower-skilled jobs were much more likely to be phased out in the coming decades, and only higher-skilled workers would be able to command better wages.

America's Digitalization Divide
https://www.citylab.com/equity/2017/11/americas-digitalization-divide/546080/
A new study maps digital-skilled jobs across industries, metro areas, and demographic groups, revealing deep divides.

In These Small Cities, AI Advances Could Be Costly
https://www.technologyreview.com/s/609076/in-these-small-cities-ai-advances-could-be-costly/
A new MIT study finds that larger cities are more resilient to technological unemployment.

Digital Economy and Its Discontents: Ongoing Crisis or Precursor to Golden Age?
https://blogs.wsj.com/cio/2017/12/08/digital-economy-and-its-discontents-ongoing-crisis-or-precursor-to-golden-age/
If we examine the long term historical big picture, patterns emerge which can help guide our understanding and planning for the future, says Columnist Irving Wladawsky-

Berger.

Even Senior Executives Need a Side Hustle

https://hbr.org/2017/11/even-senior-executives-need-a-side-hustle

Today no one should rely on just one income stream. The rise of the "gig economy" has prompted much soul-searching about the future of the economy. But portfolio careers aren't only for stay-at-home parents looking to freelance a few hours a day while their kids are in school or grad students moonlighting as Uber drivers and Task Rabbits. Even senior executives who want to stay in their corporate jobs should strongly consider developing at least one side income stream, whether it's consulting, speaking, coaching, or creating some other product or service.

ANTI/WARY

Elon Musk Lays Out Worst-Case Scenario for AI Threat

https://www.wsj.com/articles/elon-musk-warns-nations-governors-of-looming-ai-threat-calls-for-regulations-1500154345

Artificial intelligence will threaten all human jobs and could even spark a war, Tesla and SpaceX Chief Executive Elon Musk told the National Governors Association, as he called for the creation of a regulatory body to guide development of the powerful technology.

PRO/OPTIMIST

Artificial intelligence will create new kinds of work

https://www.economist.com/news/business/21727093-humans-will-supply-digital-services-complement-ai-artificial-intelligence-will-create-new

Humans will supply digital services to complement AI

WHEN the first printed books with illustrations started to appear in the 1470s in the German city of Augsburg, wood engravers rose up in protest. Worried about their jobs, they literally stopped the presses. In fact, their skills turned out to be in higher demand than before: somebody had to illustrate the growing number of books.

Workers: Fear Not the Robot Apocalypse

https://www.wsj.com/articles/workers-fear-not-the-robot-apocalypse-1504631505

Automation commonly creates more, and better-paying, jobs than it destroys. In U.S. retailing, rising e-commerce employment at such companies as Amazon more than compensates for the swoon in brick-and-mortar stores.

Getting Artificial Intelligence Right

https://www.cognizant.com/perspectives/getting-artificial-intelligence-right

Artificial Intelligence must break free from the shackles of single-point solutions to amplify human capabilities on a scale that has hitherto only been imagined.

> Author's Note: I am not familiar with Cognizant, above, but in some cases, you have to ask yourself who is selling what. In some cases, consultancies have a history of seeking to analyze data in neutral ways for the open benefit of all. In other cases, agencies, companies and consultancies are selling something, and they may be "pro-AI", in part because they are selling services or helping to guide companies in deploying AI. You just have to think critically, and also be open to discussion and explanation.

WHITEPAPERS/ANALYSIS

AI and The Future of Work

http://blog.irvingwb.com/blog/2017/12/ai-and-the-future-of-work.html

"Last month I attended AI and the Future of Work, a conference hosted by MIT's Computer Science and Artificial Intelligence Laboratory (CSAIL) and its Initiative on the Digital Economy (IDE). The two-day agenda included over 20 keynotes and panels on... "

What the future of work will mean for jobs, skills, and wages

https://www.mckinsey.com/global-themes/future-of-organizations-and-work/what-the-future-of-work-will-mean-for-jobs-skills-and-wages

In an era marked by rapid advances in automation and artificial intelligence, new research assesses the jobs lost and jobs gained under different scenarios through 2030.

Direct link to substantial report PDF: https://tinyurl.com/stt-mit

(USA Today's reaction):
Automation could kill 73 million U.S. jobs by 2030
https://www.usatoday.com/story/money/2017/11/29/automation-could-kill-73-million-u-s-jobs-2030/899878001/
Sixteen million to 54 million workers, or as much as a third of the workforce, will need to be retrained for entirely new occupations. Automation could destroy as many as 73 million U.S. jobs by 2030, but economic growth, rising productivity and other forces could more than offset the losses, according to a new report by McKinsey Global Institute.

Automation could impact 375 million jobs by 2030, new study suggests
https://www.marketwatch.com/story/automation-could-impact-375-million-jobs-by-2030-new-study-suggests-2017-11-29
Vanguard's chief global economist said it was the most important trend of his lifetime. Nobel prize-winning economist Robert Shiller said it was the single-most worrisome issue about the economy's prospects going forward.

A.I. Will Transform the Economy. But How Much, and How Soon?
https://www.nytimes.com/2017/11/30/technology/ai-will-transform-the-economy-but-how-much-and-how-soon.html
(Mentions AI Index, NBER report)
Three new reports suggest that artificial intelligence can probably do less right now than you think. But by one estimation, up to a third of American workers will have to switch jobs by 2030 largely because of it.

(NBER report)
Artificial Intelligence and the Modern Productivity Paradox: A Clash of Expectations and Statistics
Erik Brynjolfsson, Daniel Rock, Chad Syverson
http://www.nber.org/papers/w24001
Systems using artificial intelligence match or surpass human level performance in more and more domains, leveraging rapid advances in other technologies and driving soaring

stock prices. Yet measured productivity growth has declined by half over the past decade, and real income has stagnated since the late 1990s for a majority of Americans. We describe four potential explanations for this clash of expectations and statistics: false hopes, mismeasurement, redistribution, and implementation lags.

Where machines could replace humans—and where they can't (yet)
https://www.mckinsey.com/business-functions/digital-mckinsey/our-insights/where-machines-could-replace-humans-and-where-they-cant-yet
The technical potential for automation differs dramatically across sectors and activities.

21 Jobs of the Future
https://www.cognizant.com/whitepapers/21-jobs-of-the-future-a-guide-to-getting-and-staying-employed-over-the-next-10-years-codex3049.pdf

TOOLS/FUTURE/ETHICS

AI Index
http://www.aiindex.org/
An "AI Index," created by researchers at Stanford University, the Massachusetts Institute of Technology and other organizations, released on Thursday, tracks developments in artificial intelligence by measuring aspects like technical progress, investment, research citations and university enrollments. The goal of the project is to collect, curate and continually update data to better inform scientists, businesspeople, policymakers and the public.

AI Advance
https://cyber.harvard.edu/research/ai/advance
On May 15, 2017, the Berkman Klein Center in collaboration with the Media Lab hosted "AI Advance," a convening of 120 community members, including faculty, researchers, students, and fellows, in order to reflect and engage on the societal challenges of AI and related technologies, forge collaborations, and start to design research programs. "Part of our job here is to figure out: what's our research agenda? What are a series of research questions that will help us understand what we should really care about in AI? And where we should put a thumb on the scale to affect the outcome?"

71

OpenAI

www.openai.com

OpenAI is a non-profit AI research company, discovering and enacting the path to safe artificial general intelligence.

Artificial intelligence doesn't have to be evil. We just have to teach it to be good.

https://www.recode.net/2017/11/30/16577816/artificial-intelligence-ai-human-ethics-code-behavior-data

Right now, public policy and regulation on AI remains nascent, if not nonexistent. But concerned groups are raising their voices. Open AI — formed by Elon Musk and Sam Altman — is pushing for oversight. Tech leaders have come together in the Partnership on Artificial Intelligence to explore ethical issues. Watchdogs like AI Now are popping up to identify bias and root it out.

GOVERNMENT/PUBLIC POLICY

Artificial Intelligence, Automation, and the Economy

https://obamawhitehouse.archives.gov/blog/2016/12/20/artificial-intelligence-automation-and-economy

Accelerating AI capabilities will enable automation of some tasks that have long required human labor. These transformations will open up new opportunities for individuals, the economy, and society, but they will also disrupt the current livelihoods of millions of Americans. The new report examines the expected impact of AI-driven automation on the economy, and describes broad strategies that could increase the benefits of AI and mitigate its costs. AI-driven automation will transform the economy over the coming years and decades. The challenge for policymakers will be to update, strengthen, and adapt policies to respond to the economic effects of AI.

Direct link to PDF:

https://obamawhitehouse.archives.gov/sites/whitehouse.gov/files/documents/Artificial-Intelligence-Automation-Economy.PDF

Economist: Carlota Perez, London School of Economics

http://www.carlotaperez.org/
Argues that governments need to take AI seriously and consider investing in sustainable technology as a way to help create new jobs.

(A research project of Carlota Perez)

http://beyondthetechrevolution.com/
Beyond the Technological Revolution is a four-year research project led by Carlota Perez. Her research explores the relationship between technology and economic development, between finance and technological diffusion and between technical and institutional change. This project aims to analyse the role of state and society in promoting and propagating innovation to generate inclusive economic growth following a crisis.

Workplace robots could increase inequality, warns IPPR
http://www.bbc.com/news/business-42493529
The government must intervene to stop automation driving up wage inequality, a think tank has warned. The Institute for Public Policy Research said robots would not necessarily be bad for the economy. However, it warned lower-skilled jobs were much more likely to be phased out in the coming decades, and only higher-skilled workers would be able to command better wages.

> I'm repeating this link here in part to show how it amplifies the arguments of economists such as Carlota Perez, who see a potentially limited window of opportunity for governments to act. It's not just individuals and companies who need to act – if you consider the consequences of most of these articles, then everyone pretty much needs to work together to have the best chance of helping society through the disruption of AI and automation.

GLOBAL/INTERNATIONAL

Indian Technology Workers Worry About a Job Threat: Technology
https://mobile.nytimes.com/2017/06/25/business/india-outsourcing-layoffs-automation-artificial-intelligence.html?module=subsection_technology

Central Banking and Fintech—A Brave New World?
https://www.imf.org/en/News/Articles/2017/09/28/sp092917-central-banking-and-fintech-a-brave-new-world

"I would like to consider the possible impact of three innovations—virtual currencies, new models of financial intermediation, and artificial intelligence. One thing is clear: we always have more data. Some estimates suggest that 90 percent of the data available today was generated in the past two years."

Do You Feel Dizzy? Next Steps

This is the end of the chapter. Don't feel bad if you feel dizzy just glancing through the links above. Maybe they have convinced you to join me in being a realist – hope for the best future, but be prepared for change.

My first recommendation is to make a habit of reading some of the articles listed in this chapter each week (as well as to start consulting some of the news sources on your own to keep track of advances). Don't worry about it, just take action by investing time. I wouldn't recommend trying to read "everything" – meaning don't feel overwhelmed. Just set aside some time to check out developments; make a habit of it. Then it's doable.

Remember, to make it easy, you can just go to http://tsunami.ai/links - there may be some differences between what's in this chapter and that page, but it may help to make it easier. Otherwise you can google for some of the topics and headlines listed above – that could be interesting too, including clicking on the "News" link when you are doing a search.

The second recommendation is, don't feel intimidated.

When you really look at the data listed in this chapter, you have a way to respond. I am very confident that the next few chapters are a real way to respond to all the data in this chapter.

Start out by seeking to Adapt (Good).

Then, considering trying to Adopt AI (Better). Research platforms that are coming out that use AI to make given industries more automated, to assist workers. Be familiar, consider adopting, in part, to see if you can be the one who is managing AI. I fully recognize that some would choose to reject this idea, but I think it's part of being a realist. When you really look at the data, do you think you can somehow avoid AI? If you reject the idea of having anything to do with AI, consider the questions at the beginning of this chapter in the Pessimist section again – maybe you really do believe that you should do everything you can to delay, regulate and reject AI – but if you look at what happened to prior attempts to do similar things, in the auto industry, in other industries, I think history suggests that being a realist is a good perspective. Let's say that you still believe that AI is very dangerous – you are in pretty high level company – read the article above about Elon Musk – but his perspective is not to reject AI – it's to *engage* AI. If you consider AI to be the enemy, maybe it's better the enemy you know (by adopting AI), than the one you don't know. Anyway, read about Elon Musk, about OpenAI, and consider his perspective, if you are a pessimist and aren't sure whether "adopting" is for you.

Finally, I'd seriously consider seeking to become Adept in AI (Best). I'd recommend reading this book, reading articles, looking at the resources and suggestions for next steps, taking a deep breath, and diving in. I believe that this is ultimately the best form of action you can take, and that's the flow of the next few chapters. Think of them like layers, or levels: Adapt, Adopt, Adept. If you are convinced by the data to take action, and you are ready to go, start working on adapting, build the habit of learning. Seek opportunities to Adopt, make a plan.

And then consider making a plan to become an Adept – as soon as possible.

Why as soon as possible? Consider the fact that most of the articles above were in the past year from the time of writing. It's a strong indication that things are moving, and moving fast.

Also, don't ever feel you are alone – you've got me, and many other people to go along on the journey. Remember the goofy advice in the last chapter, about the key, compass and telescope? I really do believe it's possible to be optimistic about some areas (try researching the potential impact of AI on health and discoveries that could help heal chronically ill people). And I also believe that it's possible to recognize and celebrate that there is a community you can join, who are going on the same journey.

Welcome! Onward ho! Adapt, adopt, adept!

Chapter 4 - Level 1: Adapt

To review, these are the three suggested options for responding to AI, which we'll discuss over the next few chapters:

1. Adapt (good): learn more and pay attention; keep aware of where things are headed
2. Adopt (better): adopt AI-related tools and platforms, so you can be involved in managing AI
3. Adept (best): get directly involved with developing AI, by learning coding and how to work with related data

This chapter is about what it means to Adapt.

It's all about priorities.

Adapt = Wait and See

It's a good principle to be cautious; in the case of AI, hopefully you've read Chapter 3, and you're convinced to start taking action. Part of the reason for this book is to suggest practical ways of putting good intentions into action, and I firmly believe that the principles in this chapter will help you to wake up and get going in the world of AI.

In the last chapter, there was a link to an article that was very unlike most of the articles that you see about coding these days – the coder wasn't really saying you shouldn't learn to code, he was just addressing the fact that it takes work. And learning about AI definitely takes work, but in my own experience, even when I was ready to learn more, even when I was ready to put some work into it – other things just kept getting in the way.

You may be a self-starter and already capable of instantly jumping into action; that's a great quality, and a great exercise of will and determination. Other people, like me, take time to get going, and sometimes it's because of having many other things going on. But these days, exactly because of AI, there are so many things to distract you, it can be hard to be pro-active, rather than reflexive.

For example, chances are you have a Smartphone. The question is, who is in control? You, or your smart phone?

If you think you are, chances are you're not. Try giving it up for an entire day. Or try not compulsively picking it up all day, or just ignoring it. That's how closely phones are becoming intertwined with our lives, and it's helpful to note that AI, recommendations, a lot of the processing power goes into figuring out how to optimize phones, apps, social networks, and everything else that is competing for our attention. (If you want to read a provocative book about it, try The Shallows)

The bottom line is that it is harder than you think to get anything accomplished without being distracted. Studies show the quality of work, thinking, etc., is definitely better when there is space for reflection and focus; those are typically the times when you develop insight – like the kind of conviction that allows you to prioritize something like AI and actually make changes in your life to pursue it. So if you're up for it, I'd definitely recommend making a blog about it, to share your thinking with others (Ex: on blogger.com or medium.com), because there is increasing interest these days; you don't need to be an expert, you can just share your journey.

Or for that matter, some scientists have researched how the physical act of handling a book, or notebook, and writing things down, by hand, can help the learning process. Make an AI diary – that would be a great idea.

So maybe keep the blog or diary or journal in mind, and have a healthy respect for how hard it is to spend time when there is so much distraction around you.

Ok so, given the challenges, how do you take things to the next level?

How to Go from Passive to Active

I'm not an expert in motivational psychology, I'm just speaking from the experience of how hard it was to build momentum, in spite of my good intentions, to learn more about AI. For me, it was start, stop, get convicted, see a headline, ignore it, try to bury my head in the sand, set it aside, hope for the best, read another headline, decide to take a step further. And so on.

The picture earlier of the viewer at a park is supposed to represent passive watching – it's a fixed location. There's some action possible, but it's still kind of passive. And this chapter recognizes that Adapt is the starting point for just about everyone – wait and see, and maybe something triggers you into action, maybe it doesn't. I called Adapt "good", because trying to grow and learn and respond is better than nothing. At least you're more aware than you were. All I'm saying is, don't get comfortable – at this stage, I recommend being more pro-active, where you are getting up and actually pursuing some things.

So how do you make time?

Well, if you're a self-started, great. Go! And don't be surprised if you come back six months later and realize you had difficulty getting going. That's what happened to me. It took me almost a year; but one of the things that I was doing was reading articles, and becoming slightly more pro-active in reading them.

For, this, it may require proactively building a (good) habit.

Build a Habit: Practical Makes Perfect

I have found over time that for me, Google Calendar has been a helpful tool to help me build habits, with a simple feature called notifications. For a variety of reasons, I use Gmail – good spam filtering, free, a number of helpful integrated applications where with a single gmail address you can sign in and use tools like blogger.com, google sites, google docs (G Suite), and more. If you haven't tried it, I highly recommend it, and you can start by going to http://mail.google.com and making a gmail address.

Then, if you want to try this helpful little feature, sit down and go to Google, sign into Gmail, and go to the upper right hand corner of the screen with the little grid icon, click on it, and then choose Calendar:

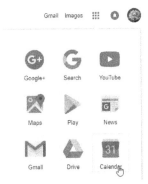

Or just go to http://calendar.google.com

Note: there's also an app, Google Calendar, and your calendar can sync, so that the reminders get to you on your phone. Amidst all the other distractions and options, it may be a good idea to try this, to help you remember things you want to remember, such as setting aside time to read, study, learn, try, etc.

In Google Calendar, you can make an appointment, and have it serve as a reminder, sending you a notification on your computer screen or Smartphone, or sending you an email. And you can make it repeat, so that each week, or day, etc., you get a reminder. You can click on the calendar directly to make an appointment, or on the +button.

Then you can click to add a title, and the magic practical feature can be found in "more options":

Then you can click on the magic does not repeat drop down menu and choose an option for how often you want the reminder to repeat.

Then if you like you can scroll down in the notification area and add or change a notification.

Tip: you can go into the Calendar settings and set up a default notification – I chose email.

Then when you're done, click the Save button.

With this magical practical makes perfect technique, you can help all your dreams to come true. Seems simple, but is helpful, especially if you get distracted, or if you ever have any trouble remembering things.

It's like training wheels for when you are learning to ride a bike. Maybe you won't need it permanently. Maybe eventually you can delete the repeating reminder – but maybe it will help you, like it has helped me, to develop a good habit. And eventually, hopefully, you won't need training wheels anymore.

And I honestly believe that time management, doing whatever it takes to build the habit of learning about AI, is the first step, helping you to become more active in learning about things.

Dig Deep for Treasure (and Motivation)

I also recommend thinking not just about where you get your information, but how deeply you dig. Over time, I recommend digging deeper. It will help give you better insight, better understanding, and stronger motivation, because you'll have a better understanding of what's going on. I believe it will help you overcome inertia, and become more active in your learning journey.

Here's what skimming the surface looks like:

I mean, ok, you've made some patterns in the sand, maybe that's art, but what about the treasure?

This is what digging deeper is like:

Ready to dig? Ok, go!

Step 1: Read Articles

Realistically, I recommend a diet of articles and books, and I'd suggest starting with articles, such as reading a few after work each day, or at least once on the weekend. Ask yourself: can you establish the habit on your own, or do you need help? If you need help, set a reminder.

Articles and Data (Ch3)

To make things easy, I recommend going through the articles from chapter 3 in more depth. Visit http://tsunami.ai/links to make it easier. Read the free ones, and see how far you can get without paying on some of the news sites. Then, I do recommend investing in NYTimes, Wall Street Journal, even MIT Technology Review. The quality of coverage is that good, and when you've read through articles I recommend, you can start reading your own – things change, things evolve. The point of this chapter is to keep up with what's changing, to become more active. Is it worth investing in? Absolutely. Can it be done for free? Yes. Have I found the additional depth, insight and analysis helpful in keeping appraised of what is going, and in hearing different perspectives? Yes. (Students, Faculty, remember that NYT and WSJ and some others have discounts).

Another thing to keep in mind is that some of those articles and studies have links on them to other resources, which are often helpful. Exploring all the rabbit trails and supporting references will definitely be rewarding, and I believe it will help you strengthen your conviction, give you knowledge and familiarity with what's going on, and help you get a good habit built.

Keep an Eye Out for Outlets

In general, here are some of the news outlets I recommend exploring:

- New York Times
- Wall Street Journal
- BBC News
- Wired
- MIT Technology Review
- TechEmergence

And by all means, go to Google and type in things like "AI news" or "Learning AI"

Step 2: Read Books

Another thing I found helpful was to build some time and space away from everything, to read a few books. For me, I prefer the paper kind of book – some studies show the physical act of turning pages can be helpful. Also, it's an opportunity to put your phone down, and to step away from your computer, and I think that's helpful, and healthy.

There are definitely many books out there; I think it's fair to go on Amazon and type in keywords you might be interested in, or even go to your library or area bookstore and go on the adventure of browsing (or in the case of the library, ask them if they have any books on AI, and if not, ask them to get some).
These three books happen to be among the first I read – the first one, Rise of the Robots, because of how someone at my local bookstore had taken the time to look through what was out there, and put some options out on

the shelves; this book looked interesting, and I read it. Then, with some other of the books, I started looking on Amazon, and I ordered more books than I actually read, which is one of my problems – good intentions, then it's hard to make the time. But eventually, I looked at the pile, and Master Algorithm seemed like it would be a nice way to get my feet wet. Then, 2nd Machine Age seemed like the next most interesting one to read.

All three of them happen to represent influential thinkers who don't necessarily agree with each other.

Rise of the Robots

https://www.amazon.com/Rise-Robots-Technology-Threat-Jobless/dp/0465097537

I'm putting Rise of the Robots first partly because I read it first, but also because I think it has a healthy dose of wariness and skepticism. The author Martin Ford probably falls in the Wary/Pessimist category, a bit like Elon Musk, but he makes a good case for his wariness, cites data, and also happens to call out some of the other thinkers and evaluate their positions, question them, and respond to them. I don't think I'm a pessimist, but I think Rise of the Robots is pretty grounded, and would be a valuable book to read and be familiar with. Along with the news articles that I was reading, Rise of the Robots, and all of the books I mention, helped me to take AI seriously, and also helped motivate me to take action.

CH1

Please forgive my odd way of quoting books; I'm going to take the pictures that I took of the book as I was reading it and include them as-is. I suppose at some point someone will convince me to turn them into "typed" text, but hopefully in this version, if you're reading it, you'll get the sense of me sitting there, and feeling that something the author said was worth capturing, important enough for me to take a picture of it for later use.

> It is an era that will be defined by a fundamental shift in the relationship between workers and machines. That shift will ultimately challenge one of our most basic assumptions about technology: that machines are tools that increase the productivity of workers. Instead, machines themselves are turning into workers, and the line between the capability of labor and capital is blurring as never before.

I think the point is important: the possibility that AI and robots can not only assist workers, but become workers. Even a complete optimist would recognize that this is happening, and will continue to happen.

This next section also got my attention, naming the likelihood that conventional approaches may not work.

> All of this suggests that we are headed toward a transition that will put enormous stress on both the economy and society. Much of the conventional advice offered to workers and to students who are preparing to enter the workforce is likely to be ineffective. The unfortunate reality is that a great many people will do everything right—at least in terms of pursuing higher education and acquiring skills—and yet will still fail to find a solid foothold in the new economy.

I don't take the prediction as a given, but I think it is an important question: are you, am I, are we pursuing the right skills?

Then economically, I think this is a fair and striking point as well:

> Jobs remain the primary mechanism by which purchasing power gets into the hands of consumers. If that mechanism continues to erode, we will face the prospect of having too few viable consumers to continue driving economic growth in our mass-market economy.

I might frame it as a question, and in particular I think of a transition already underway like Amazon. Amazon delivers value, and good prices. The little local bookstore I like in our area happens to be across from an Apple store, otherwise it might not even exist, because of Amazon. And when you walk in the door, they have a poster that questions the value of Amazon – value to the individual purchaser, but how does it affect the economy?

And my instincts tell me, that there are definitely economic forces that are causing more imbalance in wealth in societies around the world, where forces like the rise of ecommerce has replaced local retail jobs, and has offered value, to consumers and shareholders and employees – but has it helped overall to maintain or increase purchasing power? Some studies would indicate that Amazon has destroyed far more many jobs than it has created, but just like you, I use it all the time. I don't judge Amazon any more than I "judge" AI: but I think it's worth asking the question of where things are headed. And some of the data out there indicates that the middle class is weakening, that its purchase power is weakening, and that if you let this trend continue, the question becomes: will we run out of purchasing power?

I'm not an expert economist but the above trend, which AI is connected to, suggests that the environment will become more competitive. And for those of you in government, or who might answer the Realist question in Chapter 3, by saying, yes, we should advocate for change: I would read Martin Ford's book, take it seriously, seek opposing viewpoints, and join the discussion. With learning AI in particular, and with societal change in general, just letting things roll along passively is probably a bad idea. That much I believe.

So I'm just going to scratch the surface of Ford's book – it's good, worth reading. If any of the quotes above were helpful, consider that there's an entire book to read. I strongly urge you to consider buying it and reading it, or getting your library to get it and all the other books I mention. In some cases you may be able to borrow it electronically too. But I invite you to try the paper version. Take a break from your phone.

In a future edition of the book I will include book reviews at the end, and at some point I'll put the complete set of notes that I made for each of these three books, the first three chapters of each, on http://tsunami.ai

Master Algorithm

https://www.amazon.com/Master-Algorithm-Ultimate-Learning-Machine/dp/0465094279

It's really interesting the impact that Master Algorithm had on me. I already had an inkling that it would probably be a good idea for me to learn more about AI, and possibly even to learn about some of the platforms coming out, where you can leverage AI without necessarily needing to code. And part of me was intimidated, but daydreamed about being directly involved in AI, as I read about how important that task is becoming. Eventually these thoughts gelled into the idea of Adapt, Adopt, Adept – but at that point it was just swirling around in my head, and I was alternating between feeling overwhelmed by the change, and wondering if I could join the AI revolution. As I learned more about the potential AI has to replace jobs, I had mixed feelings about it, but as the Realist in me began to emerge, I felt the first hints of conviction of the inevitability of AI, and hence a sense of conviction of going from "how could I ever do that", do "how could I ever not do that".

Part of the impact that Master Algorithm had on me was surprisingly, to capture my imagination. It's partly because I respond to story, and history, and humor, and a sense of inclusiveness.

Prologue

I think the Prologue is worth reading, and it does a good job of introducing how machine learning algorithms are affecting things all around us, behind the scenes. The author discusses this, and then makes the case for the importance of machine learning, and mentions the "five tribes" of machine learning that he will be talking about in the book. I appreciate how he introduces the topic, talks about the different audiences, and is inclusive, inviting readers to consider how they might get involved and help improve machine learning to have a positive impact on the human race.

If Rise of the Robots is wary, then the Master Algorithm is optimistic, and realistic. It's also egalitarian, and recognizes how crucial it is for people to get involved from all different backgrounds, who may be able to bring insight that could make a real difference.

Good stuff.

This statement helped me to have a better understanding of machine learning, and I think it's a helpful example of what machine learning is: prediction.

> Science's predictions are more trustworthy, but they are limited to what we can systematically observe and tractably model. Big data and machine learning greatly expand that scope. Some everyday things can be predicted by the unaided mind, from catching a ball to carrying on a conversation. Some things, try as we might, are just unpredictable. For the vast middle ground between the two, there's machine learning.

I also agree 100% with this next statement, and it should probably be repeated in the chapter about being Adept.

> You can't control what you don't understand, and that's why you need to understand machine learning—as a citizen, a professional, and a human being engaged in the pursuit of happiness.

In other words, you can be passive, and maybe you'll get lucky, but it would be much, much better to be actively involved with AI and understand it.

CH1

I think this is a good realist statement, which recognizes the vast competitive advantage that a company using AI has, compared to one that doesn't.

> In the same way that a bank without databases can't compete with a bank that has them, a company without machine learning can't keep up with one that uses it. While the first company's experts write a thousand rules to predict what its customers want, the second company's algorithms learn billions of rules, a whole set of them for each individual customer. It's about as fair as spears against machine guns. Machine learning is a cool new technology, but that's not why businesses embrace it. They embrace it because they have no choice.

And it's a good summation – all the reading I've done supports it. And it's one of those things that to me points to what might be called the "inevitability" of AI, in terms of its adoption. Anything that provides competitive advantage drives adoption.

I tend to be friendly – in some ways I'm an idealist. With all I know about history, I still wish that we could all just get along. I do think that collaboration results in greater advances that people working in isolation, and sometimes I'm shy about competition. I don't want there to be losers, per se.

But let me be an idealist and realist at the same time, and take my own medicine about approaching AI as a journey, and even as a game. I play games all the time where there are winners. And I also recognize that in the business world, and with economies, that those who adopt AI first will gain the most. So yes, it's a race, it's already going on, and that's why I wrote this book, to help you recognize that it is a race, and that you should get going, as soon as possible.

> The same dynamic happens in any market where there's lots of choice and lots of data. The race is on, and whoever learns fastest wins.

So learn as much as you can, as fast as you can. Agreed.

At times, the Master Algorithm went above my head; but once in awhile it made me laugh, and it was the first thing that actually inspired the part of me that was just getting acquainted with the field, to actually want to *join in*.

I felt alternately intimidated and inspired while reading it – and sometimes it really did go over my head. My best advice for reading it is don't worry about trying to understand everything in it – just keep going, and try to get a sense of the heart of what's happening with AI and machine learning.

To me the most interesting part of the book is the sense of history you get, in terms of various approaches, their strengths and weaknesses, and the idea of somehow putting them together. In terms of data, it feels a bit like a space adventure, recognizing that a lot of progress has been made, but there's a need for more progress, and that the field is open to anyone who wishes to join it.

The funny thing is that the book inspired me to sign up for a free online course in machine learning, by one of the leaders in the space, Andrew Ng. When I saw the description for the course, it didn't seem to have pre-requisites, and I thought, ok, I'm just going to dive in! I made the mistake of also paying for the course, not realizing that you can audit it (it's available through Coursera). And then when I started taking it with the Coursera app on my phone, I realized it really was over my head – and when I found the pre-requisites, they included things that I didn't have: knowledge of statistics, probability, linear algebra, and programming in a language like Python. Part of me knew that such things are part of machine learning, but I thought perhaps it would progressively go into them. This is not the case.

So I was greatly discouraged. I was so excited! And then the notion of getting to the Adept level seemed so far away. But if it's any encouragement if you feel you could end up in a similar position, over time my enthusiasm and conviction built up again, and the very next thing I'm doing after writing this book is to register for a set of courses in Basic Programming on udacity, another learning platform.

I tell this story mainly for readers who might read the book, be inspired, and then get discouraged. What I'd say is, join me in accepting the reality that in some cases, you may need a foundation. But has my conviction about the importance of AI gone away? Nope, I'm convinced enough of the importance – important enough to finish this book, for you, before I launch into my next phase of learning.

So I would highly, strongly recommend reading Master Algorithm. Even if you have zero intention of getting involved – it really is pretty interesting, and I definitely felt like I had a better understanding of what's going on, how it works – a better understanding of the field, the importance and the potential.

2ⁿᴰ *Machine Age*

https://www.amazon.com/Second-Machine-Age-Prosperity-Technologies/dp/0393350649

The Second Machine age is the third book I read, and though I'm not going to quote it here, I think it's worth mentioning, both to get acquainted with the authors, and also as an example of an optimistic look at the future. Like Rise of the Robots, it talks about the context, and the background, but its tone is more realistic. I'd strongly recommend reading it, and then coming back to Chapter 3 and taking a closer look at some of the articles that mention things the authors are involved with. I'd also recommend re-reading Rise of the Robots, after reading the Second Machine Age. And then see where you fit in.

One of the things that's interesting to me is how the authors are optimist, but they still make disclaimers, and in the most recent edition, they specifically call out how surprised they were by advances since the previous edition.

If you like Machine Age, you may also want to read their most recent book, Machine Platform Crowd. But I still think 2nd Machine Age is worth reading.

Conclusion

I don't always include conclusions in chapters, but I am in this one, partly not to state the conclusion, but to ask you, have you come to any conclusions?

As I started reading articles and books, it gradually helped me to come to the conclusion that not only should I continue to keep AI on my reader, but I should continue to learn more, and ideally go from being passive, to becoming more active. If you like you are invited to connect with me on LinkedIn, and to see some of the articles that I wrote, as my convictions were starting to grow. http://linkedin.com/in/tekelsey

I hope you come to the conclusion that it's within your power to set aside time to invest in learning more, and to make a habit of it. I hope you conclude how important it is to do so: things move so fast with AI, that if you didn't read the news, there could be huge announcements that you miss, that have implications. It's just the way things are. In order not to get overwhelmed, I definitely recommend keeping the time you spend on a leash: do you need to read everything, know everything? No, not really. That's why some of the publications I mention are good sources, because new developments have trickled down, and if they reach the pages of NYTimes or WSJ or the BBC, then you know it's big enough to pay attention to, and there's also a fair mix of various viewpoints, which I think is helpful.

Then sources like TechEmergence can keep a good pulse on how things are developing, as well as Wired. MIT Technology Review can sometimes feel like you are reading science fiction – sometimes it's surreal: but you can keep on the forefront of things by reading publications like that, including the impact that AI is having or will have, that hasn't trickled down into popular media yet.

And I do hope you come to the conclusion that books are still worth reading. Some of the implications of AI are pretty deep, because they may convict you, and convince you, to take AI seriously, to the point of making changes in your life: knowing that it could be hard, it's easy to let things slide, to be passive, to not take action. Don't feel bad: knowing all that I knew, it took me almost a year to get to the point of finally writing this book, when I could have probably done so a year ago, if I just went with my gut.

But the books had their impact – it helped me to get some space, to reflect, and to dig deeper into things.

Best wishes on Adapting to AI. As soon as you're ready, please seriously consider going to the Adopt stage.

And if you need reminders to build the habit of reading, don't forget to set your reminders. Do it right now!

Chapter 5 – Level 2: Adopt AI

Congratulations on reaching level 2!

If you don't have Level 1 already underway, I highly recommend it: make reading news and books into an ongoing habit. Part of the reason is to keep aware of developments that might affect you directly, or there might be something interesting to explore. Developing the habit of *adapting* to AI can give you motivation, as you see things progressing and realize the idea of *adopting* AI is worth it, and not so crazy after all. But if you haven't set aside time, or at least reminders, if it's not a habit, I'd start there, and then come back to level 2.

To review, these are the three suggested options for responding to AI, which we'll discuss over the next few chapters:

4. Adapt (good): learn more and pay attention; keep aware of where things are headed
5. Adopt (better): adopt AI-related tools and platforms, so you can be involved in managing AI
6. Adept (best): get directly involved with developing AI, by learning coding and how to work with related data

Think of them as levels, and channels. Turn them on, one by one, and leave them turned on. Think of them like cylinders in an engine. If your engine has three cylinders, you want them all firing.

It's ok to be relaxed and calm about learning AI: that's ideal; trust in the process, in the community. But relaxing to the point of not taking action is not going to work. Remember that it's a race. It's not mistake that optimists would advise you to "race with the machines".

And Pedro Domingos says it well in Master Algorithm:

The same dynamic happens in any market where there's lots of choice and lots of data. The race is on, and whoever learns fastest wins.

To me this supports the idea of being a realist: in the race to utilize AI, whatever company uses AI will have a competitive advantage, so it becomes a matter of sustainability.

Alternative = Ignore, Resist, Reject AI

The reason I wrote this book is because I care about job prospects and the careers of my students and everyone else. I'm very "pro-employment", and I'm not sure there's really anyone who is "anti-employment", but the forces of business seem to be practically inevitable, in terms of the way that new technology comes along, displaces workers, and in some cases, new job opportunities are created.

I've seen both sides of the mix, so to speak, in a variety of contexts: I have family and friends in Detroit, Michigan, which was hit very heavily not only from overseas competition, but also shifts in the economy. During the Great Recession I remember driving through areas near Detroit and feeling like I was in a war zone; I don't think it's any mistake that I stumbled upon the recording of a movie (the new version of Red Dawn), which basically took a post-Apocalyptic American economy and the downtown area I was in was literally taken over as a movie set and turned into an actual war zone.

So I'm compassionate and sensitive to the disruption of a changing economy, and I don't think there's any easy answers. I happen to believe in fair trade, and I'm not sure all the trade that is going on is fair, but I'm not sure trade war is the answer either. I'm not saying I know what the answers are for countries, but at least for individuals, I do think the a willingness to evolve is good, and can make the difference between employment and unemployment, regardless of public policy or the fortunes of a particular company.

In the interviews that I do for this book, see the advice that people give; in general the theme is: learn all you can. So I think there's a strong case to be made for neither ignoring, or resisting, or rejecting AI, but accepting it as an economic reality.

But let's say that you have the reasonable concern that adopting AI might be like letting a Trojan horse into your company.

To review, the original Trojan horse was given in ancient history as a present, and when they brought the present inside the city, a bunch of soldiers jumped out and took over the city.
https://en.wikipedia.org/wiki/Trojan_Horse

Oops!

But the argument for adopting AI is a *realist* argument, and it goes back to the evidence, information, and data that you can see in Chapter 3 – not only the original articles, but also all the supporting data, studies and other articles that those writers reference. To me, it's pointing at *inevitability*. Medium-term, long-term, I don't believe anything can really "stop" AI, and I don't even think of it as a malevolent force. In the interview with Irving Wladawsky-Berger, you can see the concern I have about the number of jobs AI is expected to replace; and in conversations I've had people like Irving, sometimes they will say that AI is like electricity – it will power a lot of things. I think the electricity analogy is fair – new things will arise, new jobs, and sooner or later, it will become more universally available.

And if it's not clear to you yet, AI is already starting to be used, universally: in ecommerce (ex: Amazon), in most of the major social media platforms people use, in devices, digital assistants, etc. – it's already out there, people are using it. But in the next stage of adoption, it will be more clear; tools and platforms will be increasingly marketed as "AI-driven", or "powered by AI", or "powered by machine learning".

Whatever you think about Amazon, the rise of Amazon in relation to publishers, and the whole idea of ebooks in particular, is a good case in point. The rise of ebooks and Kindle is mainly about Amazon, but it's also about how other companies came out with e-readers. And at first, publishers were rightly wary about Amazon; some resisted developing ebooks – but very few publishers still resist the idea, and those that do are probably fairly limited in terms of growth and sustainability: Amazon came along, it has power, and it's the primary marketplace for books, and people like the Kindle, so if you don't have an ebook version of a book, it's a problem. It's the same thing with being on Amazon – as a publisher, manufacturer, or any other kind of entity; for better or worse, Amazon has the power, and if you ignore, resist and reject Amazon as an outlet, you are losing a significant source of revenue.

I don't claim to know what's right for every company or publisher in regards to Amazon – I've seen what competition between Amazon and Walmart can do to manufacturers for example: it can be a race to the bottom where you sell on Amazon, and then end up being under pressure to lower your prices because of price wars, as well as the business practices of companies like Amazon and Walmart – it's called the "Walmart Price", or, the "Amazon Price" – it's the price they make you sell your products at.

These kinds of dynamics have put some companies out of business.

So is it possible that companies, publishers who resist, reject or ignore Amazon are justified? I'm not so sure. In some ways, it's not the companies themselves, it's consumers. The little bookstore I like locally is fairly adamant in appealing to people to consider buying locally: I happen to believe in that principle. I'm not a hypocrite and I don't judge anyone, because I still shop on Amazon; and economically speaking, I think there are serious issues you get into when you weaken the middle class, and when many jobs are lost to larger companies who succeed based on things like "delivering the best price to consumers". I'm not sure it makes sense to resist or reject the companies, but I do happen to believe in the idea of shopping local.

And I think the discussion is important to consider, because the stakes are high. The numbers can float by, but if you actually look at some of the numbers mentioned in chapter 3, we're talking about hundreds of millions of jobs around the world; it's no joke.

So again – does it make sense to resist AI? I actually asked myself that question this entire year, and my sense is that sooner or later, because of economic competition and past precedents, that AI will be increasingly adopted. If AI is electricity, there may indeed by "AI Amish" people. The Amish people in America for the large part reject electricity itself – they use horses, and pretty much live around farming. An Amish family actually bought my grandfather's dairy farm, and I think there are lessons to be learned from the Amish

So anyone who chooses to be AI Amish – I respect that. But unless you go the whole way and reject all technology and become traditional Amish, I'm not sure that rejecting AI will do anything except hurt your economic prospects, that's all I'm saying.

Let's look at one last thing – would adopting AI platforms be letting a wolf in among sheep? Would it potentially hasten the demise of peoples' jobs, or a company?

I've been asking myself this particular question around the type of platform referred to as Robotic Process Automation, which can in some cases literally replace job functions. This would be from a company like WorkFusion (www.workfusion.com), which you can read about in Martin Ford's Rise of the Robots. So one approach to robotic process automation is to hold off using it as long as possible – keep as many people employed as possible using traditional techniques. And I think the question to really ask is – is that sustainable?

Resisting, rejecting, ignoring may be sustainable on a small scale, in the short-term, but in some ways, paradoxically, I think it could be like choosing defeat. A company may reject it at the expense of it helping that company to be sustainable in the long-term. I certainly don't have a blind belief that AI can do everything – it feels a bit like there will be some situations where people will prefer human-made, home-made things, and some commentators talk about this. Kind of like the Amish families who come from Indiana for a weekend farmer's market where I live in Illinois. They bring their wares, and they will probably ignore AI, and be none worse for the wear. But I'm not sure everyone can be Amish, or AI Amish, so I think that healthy wariness and caution is good, but after a year of struggling, I've come to the conclusion that I do believe launching in as quickly as possible, is probably going to be the best thing, for most people.

For companies in particular, even with something like robotic process automation, (deep breath), I'd recommend seriously looking at it. For management in an enterprise corporation that is making decisions amorally by the numbers, then this question is moot: they're going to do it, and they are starting already. For a company where sustainability includes loyalty to employees, then I do think there's something to be said for what I might call "sustainable transition" with AI: be on the forefront of adopting it, help redevelop your entire workforce, and join the race to keep as many of your employees as possible, and put all your heart and soul and mind and strength into it, so that not only can you be competitive, but so you can *grow*, and hire more people.

And if you as an individual or company are telling yourself "sounds nice but no way, not in my industry, I'm just a _____". And let me stop you right there. Take a look into a little company called Bit Source, which is comprised of coal miners who learned how to code. If I can learn how to code, so can you. I'm planning on it. If a coal miner can learn how to code, so can you.

I think that sustainable transition to AI can be done in an open transparent way that could satisfy the most compassionate manager; and I think if you look at the numbers, the transformation and disruption of automation is pretty much inevitable. Personally, I don't even necessarily take it for granted that governments will strengthen safety nets, even though I happen to believe in the interdependence of all people, to the point where I believe no one should go hungry, or be without healthcare, or shelter. I would like governments to strengthen safety nets, but I also believe in business growth, and I think the best solution to helping people who are in trouble, is through strengthening private safety nets – that's why I gave a TEDx talk on the idea of a stock exchange for non-profits: www.rgbexchange.org – strengthen private safety nets, and there's less need for taxation. Win win.

But I gave that TEDx talk over five years ago, and it's been hard to develop or find funding; that may be more of a statement on my ability than the availability of funding, but the lesson to me was: don't ask people for money, try to make it yourself. So I still believe in that vision, but I'm not holding my breath for regulation or private safety nets, for universal basic income or negative tax as some kind of balance or solution to AI. When you start looking at the numbers, then you realize why people are talking about things like that. If you have no idea of what I'm talking about, go back into Chapter 3, read all the articles, and the studies, and then look up universal basic income and negative tax, and "robot tax" – I think it would be interesting if it happened, but I don't see it happening realistically.

And this entire section is basically a way of saying "yes, I've thought it through", and "yes, I do believe adoption of platforms is the best way to go". It's not an easy question when it comes down to peoples' jobs, and a caution or wariness is definitely understandable. When I first learned about how far WorkFusion had come, and the growth prospects of the Robotic Process Automation market, I felt a sense of dread, thinking about the mass unemployment of the Great Recession.

But my journey has included becoming a realist, and I think it's a valid perspective. So there are two ways of looking at AI platforms, or companies like WorkFusion: as a threat, or as an opportunity. And in my opinion, the best way to think of them is indeed as an opportunity. You might want to look at their site, just to see. If you haven't read Rise of the Robots – read the book, then come back to their site, and you might look at it in a different light. Read the studies about 100 million people losing their jobs, and that might add another filter to the lens if you look at WorkFusion. But then, if you agree being a realist is a good idea, then you might want to go back to the WorkFusion site and go through their Automation Academy program.

So yes, I really do believe it is a good thing to *adopt*, all things considered. Not to hasten unemployment, but in recognition of the eventual adoption of AI, and in the spirit of competition and evolution, so that a given company can be at the forefront, be more competitive, and hopefully employ more people, not less. And as an individual, I believe the same thing. I want to inspire my students to hopefully seek to become people who adopt AI platforms, and are hopefully be in a position to *manage* AI.

Adopt = Adopt Automation

Now let's get back to automation. Even Robotic Process Automation is not really at the point where you can just click on one thing and then a person's entire job is automatically done. I will say that in some sectors, it is headed in that direction, depending on how routine work is, but we're not there yet.

And to understand automation, I think it's helpful to step back and consider routine work, and I'll tell a couple short stories to illustrate the point, in the context of my native field, digital marketing, which is probably especially ripe for more sophisticated automation.

If you read earlier in the book, I mentioned how I was a full time musician and I tumbled out of a tour bus and landed in a cubicle at a startup. And I had used computers, had made web pages, but I wasn't really a "coder", and frankly I felt a bit intimidated by coding: it was too abstract for me.

Routine Work is the Mother of Automation

I worked at this company, and even though it was a startup, some of the work I was doing was really boring.

I was doing the same thing, over and over and over again. Part of what was going on for me is something like the five stages of grief, where the final one is acceptance: I had to accept that I was almost famous, and working in a cubicle. That was harsh. But acceptance is good, I'm suggesting that you too, work on acceptance, as you consider choosing to pursue AI, or if you ignore it, and someday you have no choice.

I'm not suggesting that you accept boredom; I didn't: I started thinking about ways to automate the tasks I was doing. Ultimately it involved asking my colleague Ken for some help in the finer points of learning a Web language called Javascript, and I ended up making a few tools that saved me a lot of time. It freed me from drudgery and it was great. I still worked in a cubicle, but at least I wasn't as bored; I was learning, and evolving.

Later, in another job, I got to work on some marketing material in different languages. I found that exciting, but there ended up being a lot of routine work. I remembered how sometimes there are ways to automate things, and in the new situation, it involved using a feature in Microsoft Word called "macros", where you can record a series of repetitive tasks, and automate certain things with the click of a button.

That was cool. Not only did it free me from drudgery, but it felt like innovation.

Bam! Pow! I was king of the world! It was a very small world, but if you have ever had to do monotonous repetitive tasks, you know how nice it would be to escape that.

Exploring some of the features in MS Word also helped me to discover a language called VBScript, where you could take a macro and tweak it a bit. And my gradual entrance into coding has in some ways been a repeat performance of these situations, a kind of formula that anyone can follow: ask a friend to help you, or use a program that writes code for you, and then look at what's going on, and try tweaking it. Learn to make small changes to existing code, in order to get familiar, and then eventually you can learn to do it yourself.

It's funny to me to come full circle and write a book about artificial intelligence, and to realize that some of the first exposure I had to automation is because I was a bored musician just off the tour bus, working in a cubicle.

The main point is, it's not the same for every industry, but in general, routine work is a good place to start looking for opportunities, tools and platforms that could make someone's job easier. And optimists would celebrate this principle: AI will free us to be more productive. As a realist, I still think a lot of jobs are going away, and I think it's a good thing to keep in mind. But I've also witnessed first hand that when a company is growing, you need every person you can get – so maybe there's a place for optimism when it comes to automation.

Adopt = Advocate

If it hasn't occurred to you yet, you may need to *advocate* for AI, or at the very least for a company you work at to take AI very seriously. I think the principles of adapting, adopting or becoming adept hold true for both individuals as well as companies, but in a time of transition, individuals may need to be the ones to speak up about what's happening. Which means you.

You can think of data as your megaphone.

This is partly why I invite you to dig deep for data, including studies like the ones I point to, and data that the articles point to in turn. If you haven't learned the magic of letting data speak for itself, give it a shot.

Your audience may or may not be receptive.

You might even end up in a debate, where someone's passion or ability to speak may carry the day.

But when you are armed with data, you can let the data speak for itself. Data like where AI is headed in general, or doing research on the trends in particular industries (ex: from keeping track of sources like TechEmergence or through Google searchers). And hopefully you can start a thoughtful discussion.

AI is Not Just Automation

AI is not just automation. There's a lot of pretty exciting things going on. You could fill in the blank in this next picture with just about anything, starting with

"Did you hear how they used AI to . . . . "

And there's a lot of interesting, exciting things going on. Deep space

exploration, advances in science and the medical world, just about anything you can imagine. In general, the greatest uses so far have been situations where all the gadgets and devices and technology out there has been gathering a great deal of data, and the data has been so complex that it's been hard to figure out what to do with that. In certain kinds of data, machine learning has been making it vastly easier to process the data.

AI really is a key, which is poised to unlock a lot of things.

So when you're thinking about adopting AI at a company, it's not just to "make things faster", it's just that automation is one of the many things that AI and machine learning is being used for. Just remember that innovation is tied closely to AI, and no matter where you work, there may be a way to use AI for something truly extraordinary that's never been done before.

Best wishes exploring AI, and advocating for it!

AI and Existing Platforms

The platforms and devices that are developed for particular fields are going to vary wildly between industries, but a common theme would be data: the more the better, whether it's currently there in a database, or it's starting to flow in because of a system or software, or it's possible to get more data if you implement x, y and z.

I'm just going to use marketing as an example. I think it's important to consider self-driving cars, and rockets, and even robots when you're talking about AI, to capture the imagination, but marketing is also a field that's going to be impacted by AI in a big way. It's no mistake that one of the leaders in the use of AI already is Google, and it's no mistake that this year, they declared themselves as an "AI-first" company. That might be a good thing for any company to declare – and then follow through on. Likewise, China declared themselves as an AI-first *country*.

Back to Google – the reason Google is one of the largest companies in the world is the same reason that marketing is critical for any company. Though it's not quite like flying with Elon Musk in a rocket to Mars, marketing can be exciting – especially when you see the revenue come in from it. And Google figured out one of the best ways to help companies all around the world to make money in a new way – where you could actually track the results of advertising. If you type in a phrase on Google, and you see a little ad – that's worth 60 billion dollars a year to Google, and probably trillions of dollars to the companies who are running ads on Google (and Bing, and Facebook, etc.)

In the classes I teach on Google Adwords, students learn about how to make ads on Google, and one of the things that prompted me to consider learning more about AI is realizing that the potential it had to automate marketing, and when I realized how quickly things were moving, and how powerful machine learning had become, I started looking for evidence that digital marketing itself could be "highly-automated". There are already platforms around that simplify the process of working with Google ads, including automating routine work, and allowing a company to run more complex ad campaigns. For adwords, this would be platforms like Marin, and Kenshoo, called "bidding automation platforms", where companies with enough to spend can automate the process of working with many keywords and bids – part of the adwords universe.

We might think of that as marketing automation. And marketing automation can definitely come in handy, even for a small business, in things like following up with leads. For more information about that level of automation, see a book I wrote called "Intro to Marketing Automation". This level of marketing automation is sophisticated, but it's not necessarily driven by artificial intelligence; it still requires a lot of management.

Part of the reason I mention this kind of platform is because you might be on the look out for tools and platforms in your industry that allow you to gather or work with data in a semi-automated way. If such tools are not AI-driven yet, they probably will be – you could help with that, or keep your eyes out for it. And experimenting with existing tools and platforms that have automation could help you learn, and help a business to move faster and transition into the world of big data. If a business did nothing more than that, it could be competitive and sustainable, but the next level is much more sophisticated.

Intelligent Automation Platform Example: Optmyzr

Optmyzr is an interesting example of an Adwords tool that already had automation in it, which is starting to tap into the more powerful potential Google has to automate things. Google is providing artificial intelligence and machine learning tools, and has some "API's", which allow developers to connect to Google and make use of machine learning, etc.

Without getting too deep into the details, at this point anyone can sign up for a free trial of optmyzr, at www.optmyzr.com

And in this case of using an automation platform, it is linking to another tool, which is Adwords.

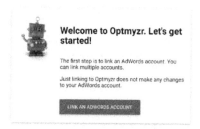

Welcome to Optmyzr. Let's get started!

The first step is to link an AdWords account. You can link multiple accounts.

Just linking to Optmyzr does not make any changes to your AdWords account.

LINK AN ADWORDS ACCOUNT

Adwords already has some automation and AI of its own going on behind the scenes, and the big question in the digital marketing industry is how long will it be before Google introduces more sophisticated AI into tools.

For this particular sector, they made an announcement in May of 2017: https://adwords.googleblog.com/2017/05/powering-ads-and-analytics-innovations.html

And it is interesting to see how Optmyzr described their implementation of this AI capability:
http://www.optmyzr.com/blog/machine-learning-improves-adwords-in-2017/

Basically they will be introducing innovations over time, and I started asking myself, based on the research I was doing – will digital marketing ever become *fully* automated? Is it even possible for digital marketing to become fully automated? And I started doing more research, searching for things like "machine learning and digital marketing", and there are some platforms starting to come out with names like Albert, that seek to automate digital marketing as much as possible, using machine learning.

I came across this article by Frederick Vallaeys, and it's a pretty good description of levels of automation, and the way artificial intelligence relate, good to read even if you aren't a digital marketer:

https://searchengineland.com/artificial-intelligence-drives-ppc-automation-267561

Frederick was employee #400 at Google, and just before the conclusion of the article he mentions this:

> *I think this is what Eric Schmidt, Google's CEO when I worked there, would talk about during our weekly TGIF meetings. He envisioned a world where the ad system was so smart that it would know how to grow any business. A company could write a blank check to Google, knowing that they would see profitable growth as a direct result.*

A reasonable question for a digital marketer to ask, when fully aware of how sophisticated AI is becoming, and knowing Google is an "AI-first" company – will digital marketers be replaced? Will companies just pay Google directly? And there's no clear answer, just like any industry. Optimists will say, AI empowers greater productivity, and indeed, Eric Schmidt, former CEO of Google, announced that AI will create more jobs than it replaces:

https://www.cnbc.com/2017/06/16/ai-robots-jobs-alphabet-eric-schmidt.html

I *hope* that AI creates more jobs than it replaces, and no one can really say how far that level of sophistication is, because advances in AI are unpredictable, a principle that is important to remember, and that no one I know of disagrees with. So I tend to think not of "if" when a certain threshold will be reached, but when. And in the meantime, there are companies and platforms starting to offer AI, such as tapping into Google (and Google working on advances all the time, which they may or may not announcement, which is also important to remember)

If we take all this into account, a practical example is Optmyzr, ready for use by anyone using Adwords, and it utilizes some machine learning; it is still an assistive tool. And such a tool could very well make your life easier.

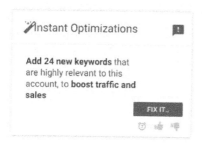

Or something like this:

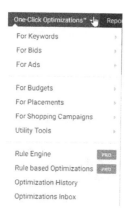

Google will surely build the capability of adwords itself, and there will be platforms like Optmyzr that people can adopt. After the research I've done, for a variety of reasons, I think it's a really good idea to not only do research on emerging tools, but to explore them and adopt them, hopefully to be competitive and on the forefront of things.

Entirely New Platforms

Many tools and systems and devices are starting to use AI in some way, and part of adopting AI is to look for those tools. One place to look is wherever a lot of data is coming in and need analysis, or new kinds of sensors or techniques are getting new kinds of data, that needs interpretation. In the physical world, sometimes this means robotics, other times it doesn't. There's no single formula, but learning about how AI may enable existing platforms and techniques is a good thing (as well as asking yourself, how could AI help with _____ and then seeing if a tool exists, and either using it, help make it better, or make something yourself, or form a company) I believe in cross pollination – one of my favorite books is Innovators by Walter Isaacson, and one of the things he discovered is how important cross pollination is in "innovation ecosystems", where some of the most interesting innovation came when people from *different fields* got together. This is why reading general science, or general news can be helpful, or looking at how things are progressing with AI, not just in your own field, but in other fields. An example of news on AI in multiple fields could be going to www.techemergence.com, and simply browsing multiple industries:

Using this approach, you might come across new platforms, or new *opportunities* for platforms. Another good publication for inspiration is MIT Technology Review (worth paying for), or the free but always interesting Science Daily News, which in addition to science discoveries, also sometimes includes how AI is being used in science (Ex: such as to help astronomers find new things and help deal with massive amounts of data). www.sciencedaily.com

And of course, Google is good for finding new platforms:

New AI-Based Tools Are Transforming Social Media Marketing
https://www.forbes.com/sites/johnellett/2017/07/27/new-ai-based-tools-are-transforming-social-media-marketing/#738262ae69a2

This New AI Platform Wants to Help More Women Entrepreneurs Become Millionaires
https://www.entrepreneur.com/article/294148

Dell, Circular Board and Pivotal have partnered to make the startup ecosystem easier -- and more profitable -- to navigate.

You can try "new AI platforms for _____" and fill in the blank, or for even more fun, learn how to create a google alert, which will send you an email about when something new comes in that fits your search.

Another general source of examples of how AI is being used is IBM's Watson. Watson is an example of a powerful AI platform in the cloud, which is increasingly being tapped into for various applications.

https://www.ibm.com/watson/

They have interesting examples of how AI is being used.

Google and Amazon also have AI platforms that they are opening up for use, and Baidu in China is doing the same thing.

Datarobot

There are a lot of new AI companies, and some of them are not just working on applying AI to a particular industry, but finding ways to make AI more accessible. Datarobot is an interesting company that is starting to do this kind of thing.

www.datarobot.com

All of these links on their home page are worth exploring, including ("we're hiring"):

As with most companies, they also have videos that are probably worth watching.

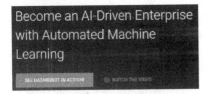

DataRobot is an example of a "general-purpose" AI platform that might help a given company to harness AI, where the person working on a project may not necessarily have to be an "expert", but could be in the process of developing *expertise*.

The "getting started with data science" is probably my favorite part, and I recommend you check DataRobot out, as you work on *adopting* AI.

Conclusion

Ok, I guess we have another conclusion. We've taken a look at various ways to explore adopting AI, including looking at platforms that can help, and general purpose platforms that may represent opportunities to explore AI and learn more about it.

As we reviewed in the beginning, there is an opportunity to not only adapt to AI, but also adopt AI, and become adept. Maybe the "channel" analogy is good. What I'm recommending that you do is to build the habit of keeping track of where things are going, and in this chapter, adding in a layer of rolling up your sleeves and "trying" AI. Depending on your field, there may be a tailor-made platform ready to go, or an opportunity to think of one and go find a company to help you make it, join a company that is making one, or start your own company.

And there's also platforms like DataRobot to explore, to help you get your feet wet – maybe it will lead to a different job at your current company, or maybe you will end up with one of those new types of jobs that AI optimists talk about, that don't exist yet, something like AI Implementation Specialist. That has a nice ring to it.

Part of the message is: start to explore, but don't stop learning and keeping track of news. And certainly, I hope you'll seriously consider reading the next chapter and acting on it. Maybe you're ready to dive in, but it's certainly ok to explore things in stages: adapt, adopt, adept. Start looking at the news, read a few books, start trying a platform or two.

But if it hasn't been clear from the discussion, there are a few things to consider: AI is increasingly rapidly in sophistication, and this has two implications: one is that no matter what platform is created, which "assists" someone, you can ask the question: "Will that management role itself be possible to automate?". And I think that adopting AI is going beyond adapting AI, and a good thing. But you shouldn't stop there, in part, because there's a reality that I think is good to accept. It may be possible to automate just about anything.

Can _____ be automated? Probably, sooner or later. I started looking at what optimists were saying, and researching, and things like creative work and writing are sometimes cited as "too hard too automate", or another phrase you'll hear, which sounds like journalists trying to re-assure themselves, "not anytime soon". But the important thing to remember is, that it's probably a question of *when*, not if. And if you look at what the experts say, it's hard to say when AI will reach a point of being able to do x, y or z. There are some articles out there that have predictions, but past predictions have been wrong; and sometimes experts have been surprised, including with advances that have happened in the past year.

For example, there's a little thing called quantum computing, which may completely surprise just about everyone, and greatly speed up how fast computers can process things . . . .like data. If you're starting to get a headache, maybe you'd enjoy reading some fiction. Try "The Quantum Spy", or look up "AI in fiction", "AI in movies", or "quantum computing in fiction", or "quantum computing in popular media"

Just prepare to be surprised. And also, please consider becoming adept. I'm trying to do the best I can to inspire you; as for me, I was inspired by the Master Algorithm. I hope you consider reading it too.

And now, onward to becoming Adept in AI!

Chapter 6 – Level 3: Become Adept in AI

Congratulations on reaching level 3!

To review, these are the three suggested options for responding to AI, which we've been discussing over these last few chapters:

7. Adapt (good): learn more and pay attention; keep aware of where things are headed
8. Adopt (better): adopt AI-related tools and platforms, so you can be involved in managing AI
9. Adept (best): get directly involved with developing AI, by learning coding and how to work with related data

Think of them as levels, and channels. Turn them on, one by one, and leave them turned on.

For this chapter especially, I'd recommend skimming it first – don't worry about understanding or even acting on it. If you're reading through the book before acting on anything, I truly believe that setting the first level in motion is the top priority. So I'm just emphasizing that you don't need to "get" everything in this chapter, but I'd use it as an opportunity to get acquainted; and then I'd come back to it and act on it as soon as you're ready.

There are some people who might be ready to launch into AI and data science after reading this chapter, but the reason for reaching the first two levels is still relevant: when you learn how to adapt to AI, you are learning how to adapt to advances in AI, and there's never really a time you should be ignoring advances. It's more the opposite, it's always important to keep an eye on advances. And you might read about things that inspire you, or give you ideas.

Similarly, no matter how "ready" you are, I think that learning how to *adopt* AI is important, because you are generally talking about platforms, and the concept of particular businesses and industries making use of AI. Keeping abreast of applications, and trying them, is important. You don't want to get too deep into theory, without being grounded in practice, and *keeping* grounded in practice. Furthermore, the adopt stage might be one where there is the most opportunity to find, or create a new job – you might find a company that wants to implement AI, you might advocate for it and be the person to lead the charge, or you might want to get a grounding in the applications of AI, as you're learning it, and you might look for a role at a company where you could use an "AI-enabled platform', in order to get experience in data science, artificial intelligence or machine learning, even as you're learning it.

So yes, it really is important to set the habit of learning to adapt to AI, learning to adopt AI, in motion, and to keep involved with each.

Adept = Develop Knowledge and Skills

When it comes to learning, I'm an optimist. Some experts may disagree with me on how "approachable" AI is, and they might question the recommendation that everyone seek to become more of a data scientist. But I've witnessed a phenomena with a number of technologies in my career, where technologies are only accessible to wizards, and then it becomes easier to use for everyone. This is an unscientific diagram, but it's something like this:

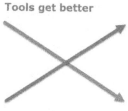

Tools get better

Less difficult to join in

And I think there's reason to believe that even if it isn't "easy" to get involved or learn AI, it will become easier, and one way to help the learning process in general is to look for "assistive" tools that make the technology more accessible. In the case of AI or Data Science, it might be a tool or platform like DataRobot, which could allow a business without a lot of AI expertise on staff to nonetheless utilize AI and machine learning. One of the factors driving this trend is the very scarcity of AI expertise these days. In my opinion, becoming "adept" in AI does mean exploring the roots, including data science, and learning the core skills so that you have a flexible toolset. No matter how far you go, the more you learn in fundamental areas, the more employable you will be, and the more you will be able to accomplish.

For some people in business, this could mean focusing on the implementation side, such as learning enough about AI to have some fluency, but keeping your eyes out for tools and platforms like DataRobot that attempt to meet you halfway, even if you don't have the coding skills or expertise in data science. At this stage, it seems like the tools are a ways off that can make AI more "democratized", because AI and machine learning necessarily involve a lot of data, and you have to know something about how to work with data in order to work with machine learning, and AI.

AI Helper Platforms

I would suggest looking at the emerging platforms as ways to assist with AI, but not a replacement for learning the core skills. As a limited analogy, you could think of web pages. These days, a tool like weebly allows just about anyone to make a web page without knowing any code. Maybe tools from

DataRobot, IBM, Google, Amazon, will someday be something like a weebly for AI. I can even imagine startups using phrases like that to pitch to a startup accelerator like YCombinator. Or the phrase "democratizing AI".

But machine learning is still more complex than a web page, by the very nature of the complexity of the data that you are dealing with, and the many forms it can come in. For limited, focused applications, assistive tools like DataRobot can go a fair ways, and will increasingly go a longer way on their own to help cut down on the knowledge and skills required – so for some, working on implementing a platform or tool like DataRobot in some ways might be at the "Adopt" stage – there's a kind of grey area between the chapters in some ways. But I'm recommending that assistive tools not be a replacement for the core skills – because the core skills can not only help you use those platforms better, but can also help you make better use of them.

We'll see how things shake out, but on your journey, take a look at some of the platforms, and if I were you, keep your eye on them, not only the big companies, but also the startups like DataRobot. Some of those startups are likely to get acquired by bigger fish, but you don't have to wait for that to be aware of them or start using them. And keeping your eyes on the news is another way to find out about such tools.

DataRobot

DataRobot is probably a good place to start. (You could also search for things like "DataRobot competitors" or "alternatives to DataRobot" and see what comes up.)

I'm impressed with what I've seen so far, at www.datarobot.com:

DataRobot   PRODUCT   SOLUTIONS   LEARNING   ABOUT   WE'RE HIRING!

Explore the site, the industries, everything. Put it on your radar, try it, keep it in mind.

For example, if you type in the phrase "machine learning for the masses", you'll see this year Amazon released SageMaker.

https://www.itworld.com/article/3239247/artificial-intelligence/amazon-web-services-brings-machine-learning-to-the-masses-with-sagemaker-and-deeplens.html

https://aws.amazon.com/sagemaker/

And Google has been working fairly hard on increasing access to Tensorflow, which is one of the popular deep learning platforms: https://www.tensorflow.org/

Tensorflow is still fairly complex, but Google also announced AutoML, a major breakthrough that was one of the reasons I wrote this book, because it basically amounts to AI programming itself.

https://futurism.com/googles-machine-learning-software-has-learned-to-replicate-itself/
https://www.wired.com/story/googles-learning-software-learns-to-write-learning-software/

https://hackernoon.com/next-disruptive-wave-will-be-automl-4b0367347ab2

AutoML is one of those things that is in the Wild West, but there could be a breakthrough at any time.

And it brings up a decent point – if artificial intelligence will just write itself, should we just give up and join the Amish? Maybe we should join the Amish, or form a new tribe of Amish that actually embrace AI, but in the meantime, even if Google announced that AutoML will write itself tomorrow, there will still be plenty of need for people to help implement, configure and create artificial intelligence, and a continued need for data scientists.

Some researchers believe that most code will be written by computers by 2040:
https://fossbytes.com/machine-generated-code-mgc-2040/

But I wouldn't worry about it; I'd just learn as much as you can, as fast as you can, in a sustainable way, and keep an eye on developments. For something like automl, chances are that if you do follow through on continuing to adapt to AI, meaning keep reading the news, that developments will be announced there, but you could also do a search on automl once in awhile.

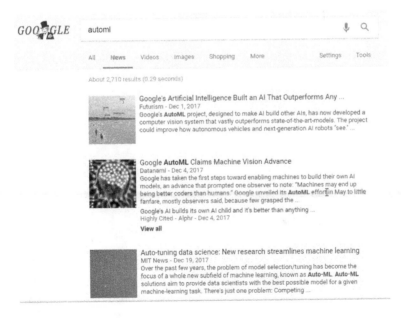

But as long as it doesn't stress you out, I'd recommend trying out Google Alerts:

Alert Yourself about Assistive Platforms

You could use Google alerts for any aspect of learning AI, but it might be fun for AutoML in particular, because of how high the stakes are, and because it would be a way to keep on the very forefront of AI, perhaps as soon as the writers in all the publications I mention. Short of being an employee at Google, it's the next best thing. (And even if you are an employee at Google, you may still want to use Google alerts anyway, in case they go right to the public with an update!)

To try Google Alerts, go to: https://www.google.com/alerts

Type in something like automl, and then the show options link:

You may want to set the timing to something like "at most once a week". Then enter your email address if it doesn't already appear, and click Create Alert. You can always go back to Google Alerts and change or delete them.

One of the reasons to explore such platforms as you're learning is because the big companies are likely to have videos and other learning material that are designer to help customers adopt their platforms. There will certainly be books as well that emerge on the topics, as the platforms mature.

IBM has been in the space actively for awhile, and also has similar goals and resources: https://www.ibm.com/information-technology/machine-learning-masses-exploration-and-discovery

Microsoft has been at it for awhile too, with their Azure platform: https://bits.blogs.nytimes.com/2014/06/16/microsoft-unveils-machine-learning-for-the-masses/

Amazon and Microsoft even partnered on a project: https://futurism.com/microsoft-and-amazon-have-partnered-to-bring-ai-to-the-masses/

And don't forget the startups like DataRobot. You never know what might happen in someone's garage.

AI = Machine Learning

In case it isn't clear by now, machine learning is a core part of artificial intelligence. As you consider learning more about AI, it's important to have that clear. It's helpful to realize that machine learning isn't the only form of artificial intelligence, but it's the one that is having a huge impact now, and is poised to have a fundamental impact for some time. How long? Who can say.

In the next chapter we'll take a look at the core concepts of AI, such as machine learning, deep learning and neural networks, for now, the important connection to make for the learning journey is the fact that machine learning plays prominently in AI. If you're ready to dive in, read Master Algorithm, discussed in a previous chapter, or visit the free learning site: http://neuralnetworksanddeeplearning.com/index.html

Machine Learning = Data Science

The next thing to check off on the list is that AI and Machine Learning relate very closely to the field of data science. Some might say that machine learning "is" a part of data science, and one way to simplify it is to think of data science as one of the areas that allows you to "apply" AI to business and other fields these days. The main reason is that in order to make practical use of AI in business, you need to be able to work with the data from that business. Another buzzword that you may have heard of is "Big Data", which is more of a media buzzword than a field, but in this book I'm sticking with data science.

App AI - Getting Started: Start with Videos (or come back to them)

One of the most interesting opportunities that I see is finding ways to simplify the process of learning about AI, and ways to make learning about AI more fun and interesting. In general, I'd say one way to keep AI concrete and not too abstract, is to keep your eyes open for ways that AI is being applied, as well as ways people have attempted to make AI more visual, including with videos. Another way is to look for ways to learn about AI with apps on your smart phone or tablet, so that it feels simpler and is more convenient.

For example, I'd suggest searching on youtube for the following phrases, either on the website, or even the app itself, especially if data and numbers are not your natural territory.

Some of these videos might inspire you and capture your imagination.

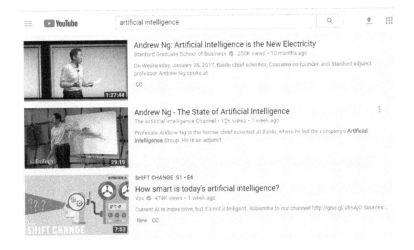

Andrew Ng is one of the leaders in the AI world, and cares about helping people to learn about AI. I think his comments about AI being the "new electricity" are worth considering.

For the ethical questions surrounding AI, and to look at opposing viewpoints, try searching for "elon musk ai":

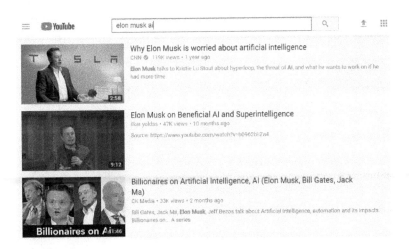

You might be interested to watch the video where billionaires weigh in on AI: they see its potential, and have already been using it.

For grins, you might also want to search for "elon musk Sophia" to see an amusing example of AI talking about one of its critics:

Elon Musk is a unique example of someone who is wary of AI but fully embraces it at the same time, in the various companies he is involved with.

As part of understanding how machine learning relates to AI, I'd search for "machine learning" on youtube and watch some or all of these videos:

And to get a sense of the very latest advances, I'd search for "deep learning":

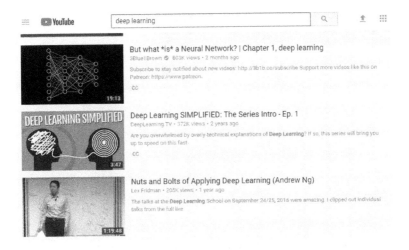

Each of the videos in these screenshots I made would be worth watching. In the above videos, you can get a sense of what a neural network is, and I think that any attempt to simplify understanding about deep learning is admirable.

Games

Let the games begin! There seem to be a few games out there that can help people of all ages to learn data science and artificial intelligence. I think there could be, should be more. (Do you know of any games? Do you want to help make one? Please check http://tsunami.ai/games to see that latest list, and use the contact form and let me know.)

These are some of the closest things I've found.

https://experiments.withgoogle.com/ai
AI Experiments is a showcase for simple experiments that make it easier for anyone to start exploring machine learning, through pictures, drawings, language, music, and more.

Play with a Neural Network
http://playground.tensorflow.org
This is a bit more advanced; I'd recommend filing it away and coming back to it, or just playing around with it.

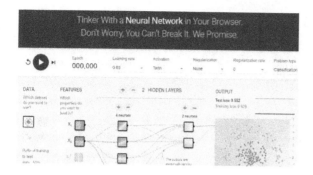

Neural Networks and Deep Learning – free online book

http://neuralnetworksanddeeplearning.com/index.html
> In the resource above they mention this book and it's actually a good thing to consider reading.

An Introduction to Neural Networks With an Application to Games

https://software.intel.com/en-us/articles/an-introduction-to-neural-networks-with-an-application-to-games
> This is more about how AI and neural networks are being used in games, but it may be interesting.

Alas the examples of game-based learning for AI are few, but I hope there are more.

Games for Learning Coding

I think there are more games out there that help with learning coding. Don't be shy! Especially if data or coding seem to far out of reach to you, abstract or boring. One thing to consider with coding especially is to try to learn how to make games with a language like Python – it might be an example of project-based learning, where you can picture an end result, or read a book on the topic and work towards an approachable goal, which might be fun to learn how to do, and to play.

In terms of games where you can actually play and learn something to try coding, I'd recommend doing a simple google search and exploring some of the options and articles.

Go gle   games for learning programming

12 Free Games to Learn Programming. – Mybridge for Professionals
https://medium.mybridge.co/12-free-resources-learn-to-code-while-playing-games-f7... ▾
Apr 25, 2016 - The selections include free, open source and freemium sites that are designed for both
beginners and advanced programmers to learn a variety of computer languages such as JavaScript,
Java, Python, PHP, C#, etc. Learn to Code by Making Games — The Complete Unity Developer.

CodeCombat - Learn how to code by playing a game
https://codecombat.com/ ▾
Learn programming with a multiplayer live coding strategy game for beginners. Learn Python or
JavaScript as you defeat ogres, solve mazes, and level up. Open source HTML5 game!
Play Now · Learn to Code! · Teacher · About

15 Free Games to Level Up Your Coding Skills - Skillcrush
https://skillcrush.com/2017/04/03/free-coding-games/ ▾
Sep 28, 2017 - CodeMonkey. CodeMonkey teaches coding using CoffeeScript, a real programming
language, to teach you to build your own games in HTML5. CodinGame offers up games to learn more
than 25 programming languages, including JavaScript, Ruby, and PHP. CSS Diner is a simple but fun
way to learn CSS.

15 free games that will help you learn how to code - Business Insider
www.businessinsider.com/15-free-games-that-will-help-you-learn-how-to-code-2017-4 ▾
Apr 5, 2017 - 2. CodinGame. CodinGame offers up games to learn more than 25 programming
languages, including JavaScript, Ruby, and PHP. One of the great things about CodinGame is that you
can play with friends or colleagues, and also enter international coding competitions. CSS Diner ...

Part of the reason that I sometimes include screenshots of google searches instead of links themselves is because of how often things changed and how new things come about.

Get Your Feet Wet – with Apps

Aside from watching videos and playing a game or two, I'd suggest considering making it as easy as possible for you to take steps forward in learning.

In my opinion, the best way to learn is in community, as you'll see later, so I do think that there are advantages to having an instructor who can mentor you. I think the structure, community and presence of a mentor who you can ask questions to is very helpful, so I'm definitely "pro in-person" in terms of education, especially for anyone who feels a sense of intimidation, or needs some help with motivation.

Having said that, I think one of the easiest ways to get started, and to maintain momentum, is through the simplicity of adding a few free apps:

1. Coursera (or Udacity, or Udemy)
2. DataCamp – Programming for Data Science
3. Khan Academy – Math

I do think it can be as simple as 1-2-3, and keeping those particular apps in view on your home screen, and building the habit of advancing in them.

Coursera (or Udacity, or Udemy)

Coursera is a popular platform for free online courses, which includes things like courses that Andrew Ng created. You can take the courses in audit mode, and you can also discover good resources for learning about AI and some of the pre-requisites, from looking at what instructors recommend in terms of learning more. The paid version of a course in Coursera can result in a certificate and additional access to resources in some cases.

For fun, you may want to try launching in to the original "machine learning" course at Coursera, taught by Andrew Ng – just don't be discouraged when you start running into some of the pre-requisites, in terms of programming knowledge. I'd suggest wandering through Coursera, Udacity, and Udemy, and see the latest offerings in terms of artificial intelligence, machine learning, data science, and some of the related skill areas, such as basic programming, Python, and math.

DataCamp

DataCamp is a nice platform for getting into Data Science. You may find it comforting and less stressful to look at a single one click app, than all of the potential resources out there in the field of data science.

If you get any sense of data science or AI being unapproachable, just download the DataCamp app.

For what it's worth, DataCamp app was recommended to me by a professor of Data Science who is brushing up on things themselves.

After you've watched some videos to help stretch and inspire your mind a bit, for some people, it may be as simple as cracking the ice and getting your feet wet with an app like DataCamp, as simple as having one icon on your precious home screen.

Give it a shot. And consider making room for Coursera and Khan Academy too.

Math: Khan Academy

Keep your eyes on Khan Academy, not only for math, but also for programming and hopefully at some point for machine learning and artificial intelligence. But for math, Khan academy is unparalleled, and free.

As you learn more about the things you need to learn more about, at some point soon I'd recommend investing time in learning more math.

These are some courses you'll probably want to consider taking
https://www.khanacademy.org/math/statistics-probability
https://www.khanacademy.org/math/algebra
https://www.khanacademy.org/math/linear-algebra

Don't Forget the Website

All the apps we've been looking at, and sometimes you get a better sense of what is going on by visiting the website. If it works for you, download the apps I'm recommending to get your feet wet and get started, but also consider taking a look at the websites. For example, I think the DataCamp website (www.datacamp.com) is important enough that I want to highlight it. It can help you get a feel for what kinds of options are possible.

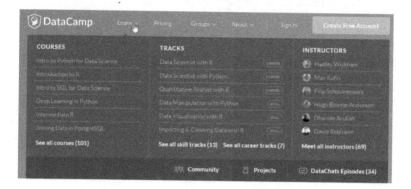

No Way, No Math, Stop, My Brain Is Melting

I get it, if you're not a math person. This might be a point where you'd want to go back to Chapter 3 and look at all the data about how important AI is. I completely understand if you look at math alone and think that there's no way you could learn more math.

But I believe you can. I doubted myself on math in the past, but I've gone through something like the five stages of grief, where the final stage is acceptance.

If you're like me, at any point in your journey from the time you are convinced of the importance of learning more about AI, you may second guess yourself, doubting your ability, or you may be drawn to reasons for dismissing the idea altogether.

To be clear, I *don't* presume that I know what's right for you. But all the data and reading I've been doing convinced me to take AI seriously, and I have come to believe it is important for everyone to learn more about data science. Everyone. And throughout the past year I had 100 different reasons to drop things, including wondering whether I'd be capable about learning more. But one of the things that convinced me to keep on going is that very phrase, which my grandpa used to say to me: "keep on going".

That's partly why I believe it's important to learn in community, even if that means finding an "AI buddy" and you both sit down each week and learn, from your phones, even if you never talk to each other. I think you'd find discussing what you learn helpful, and that you'd also find encouragement in having someone to learn from and to help keep you on track.

But ultimately it was the data that convinced me, and I hope it convinces you, even if you have to keep coming back to it. That data, and the willingness to recognize the implications, is a magic ingredient in motivation, in my opinion. Encouragement, community, those are also magic ingredients. For certain kinds of people like myself, confronting and recognizing the data can lead to acceptance, and I think that can help you go from considering learning more about things like math, to actually doing it.

Make no mistake, acceptance doesn't have to involve grief – if you're "not a math person" by nature, remember that many people who are the same have learned math, and done what they need to do to get it. You can too, I truly believe that. Acceptance can become a positive thing, because you can *choose* to move forward.

135

As for me, another magic ingredient in learning math happened to be a book that my mom recommended, who was a teacher for many years. It's called "All the Math You'll Ever Need". It came in handy when I was taking the GRE exam for getting into graduate school, after not having taken a math class for a long time.

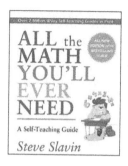

https://www.amazon.com/Math-Youll-Ever-Need-Self-Teaching/dp/0471317519

I'd highly recommend it. If you like books you might want to start there, to work on your "math channel", and then consider reading Steve Slavin's book on algebra.

https://www.amazon.com/Practical-Algebra-Self-Teaching-Guide-Second/dp/0471530123

Don't laugh at me too hard but you may want to consider going on a math vacation, where you go somewhere nice, or even just a local park, and read a book on math. Relax as much as you can, dive in a pool, and then dive into math.

Another recommended option would be exploring a community college course – or just looking at Khan Academy.

Get in Touch with your Inner Data Scientist

Ultimately, as part of becoming adept in AI, you'll want to learn more about data science.

You Already *Are* a Data Scientist

Remember, you are already using a lot of data, without even thinking about it. Data is flowing past you and around you all the time, and you are constantly taking recommendations based on data.

Part of data science is not just taking other peoples' words for it, but learning how to work with data yourself. This is part of the "big data" revolution that can help you be more competitive in the job market, and help you get involved in AI.

Avoid Overload: Think of a Project

One recommendation I have as you explore the world of data science is to try and look for opportunities to think of projects that help you learn data science. That is, if you ever end up feeling the least bit overwhelmed by all the options, learn the trick of turning the tables on complexity. You don't have to learn everything – you can learn what you need to be functional, and grow from there.

I think this is true in many fields, and books or courses that attempt to teach knowledge often end up falling into the trap of trying to be complete references. That in turn makes it harder to learn, because you lose context; the learning process can become abstract. And it's harder for the brain to form the synapses to remember things. That's one of the reasons why we sometimes end up remembering a small percentage of what we're exposed to in a course.

An example would be of how a friend was a journalist and interested in learning more about social media. They ended up understandably overwhelmed by all the tools, sites and techniques out there, and I encouraged them to focus on some of the primary ones and branch out from there, and to recognize there would be no way of learning everything. You have to start somewhere.

Another reason thinking of a project can be helpful is to help clear the fog of "technospeak". I think this can apply to self-teaching, but also when you're actually trying to implement what you learn, or use a technology tool in a business. It's especially true when you are "translating", helping people to learn about the tool you are using to help the business or organizing. Sometimes people get frozen thinking they have to necessarily understand all the options that tools can provide – sometimes that is helpful, but another way to go about implementing a tool or technology is to keep a *business objective* clear.

Defining a business objective can be helpful, because it highlights the priority of defining the value for the business. It can be easy for a business or individual to get lost in the options and technology, so it can be helpful to ask people to define the business objective as a starting point, and then look at how a tool can help you reach that objective.

I definitely think it's worth keeping in mind as a principle, when you look at books or courses – is there a project where you can do some hands-on learning? That's preferable, when possible. If you have access to an instructor, you can ask them to help you create one, even if they didn't plan that for the course.

And even if you have to start with yourself, you can ask yourself questions like:

"How could I use artificial intelligence to _____"
"How could machine learning help a business like a _____"

These kinds of questions can be helpful to ask when you can discuss it and brainstorm with others.

And it can naturally lead to data questions, like:

"What kinds of data does a _____ use?"

Or in terms of devices:

"What kinds of data does a _____ gather?"

Even if there isn't a specific project in a book, you can look at websites, including many of the ones listed in this book, for white papers and case studies, and even search for "ai case study" or "machine learning case study", and look for concrete projects where AI and machine learning was used.

And the point of asking questions is, you don't need to be an AI expert to start thinking of business objectives, or potential uses of machine learning. You can brainstorm, and think of projects, or learn about advances in AI, and imagine how AI might be able to help solve particular problems.

Don't be surprised if at some point, you end up getting excited about a particular application of AI. That might help you to have extra motivation to learn more. And don't be afraid to look for other people with the same interest. Chances are there are others who are a) trying to learn about data science and b) looking for other people to team up with. That's how learning happens. That's how startup companies form. That's how innovative teams in existing companies form.

No Way, Not Me: Rock n Roll > Data

Just in case there's anyone shaking their head, writing themselves out of the picture, remember two things:

1) There are coal miners who are learning how to code. Look up BitSource. There are countless other examples of people who made transitions.

2) If personal examples work for you, remember that it was not too long ago that I was a professional musician, and fell off of a tourbus, and here I am writing a book about artificial intelligence.

If I can do it, *you* can do it.

Exploring Coding

As you learn about data science, you'll encounter the need to learn more about coding sooner or later, and in the current state of data science, you'll come across the question of learning R, or Python, or both.

Python or R or Both?

There are people who have different viewpoints on this, but in my perspective, I'd suggest learning Python first, because of its wide applicability. With all due respect to R, I believe that there are probably more employment prospects for people with Python programming than R, including outside the field of data science.

There's no right or wrong answer, but it can end up being a question as soon as you open up an app like Datacamp, which asks you which you want to learn.

Choosing R or Python for Data Analysis? An Infographic

https://www.datacamp.com/community/tutorials/r-or-python-for-data-analysis

Python vs. R: The battle for data scientist mind share

https://www.infoworld.com/article/3187550/data-science/python-vs-r-the-battle-for-data-scientist-mind-share.html

Explore Data Science

In this section, we're going to look at data science, and some of the things I think are helpful to keep in mind as you consider learning about it.

Data Science and Business

One of the ways to think of data science is how it can help take something like AI or machine learning and make it applicable to a business. In theory, you could learn about artificial intelligence in isolation, such as "purse science", and it could be very interesting, but it's not until you start to apply it that it has more universal value. (I hope some readers do consider going into "pure research" and even getting a PhD, and joining the ranks of people like Andrew Ng, and Pedros Domingos, and other AI researchers who teach computer science. One of the big problems in AI is that a lot of talent is being taken out of academia, and there's a big vacuum forming, so there's a definite need there, and it will continue to be felt.)

Traditional Data Science Skills

I'd recommend taking some time to explore what various people consider to be top skills for data science, and to consider the context. In general, they tend to fall into technical and non-technical categories. They might involve a list like this:

(technical)
Math: the knowledge of math to work with tools
Programming: programming is often necessary to help analyze and transform data
Analysis: data can be just information, but it's important to be able to turn it into actionable insight.

(non-technical, or semi-technical)
Product/System Knowledge: this to me means understanding the ways that a business works, and the systems that a business has in place, or could have in place, for gathering, distributing and acting on data, wherever that data comes from, be it a website, or devices, etc.

(non-technical)

Communication/Teamwork: the people dimension in data science is often overlooked. You remember the mention of Harvey Mudd College in the "data" chapter – if you don't, you might want to go back and look at the related links. Harvey Mudd grads are highly sought after, because they know not only the technology, but also have developed communication skills, working with people. Suffice to say, these "soft" skills are important, and a well-rounded program of learning can and should include learning more about communication and teamwork.

Here are some articles to consider reading at some point that talk about the particulars.

--

Making Sense of Data Science: 4 Key Skills Your Data-Driven Company Needs

https://business.udemy.com/blog/data-science-skills-data-driven-company-needs/

1. Data science algorithms
2. Experimental design
3. Machine learning and deep learning
4. Wrangling big data

> *While using Python gives data scientists a lot of power and flexibility, it's possible to perform data science without Python programming expertise. The simpler R scripting language is an alternative to Python, or an analyst might even use a software package called Tableau that doesn't require programming at all.*

> This article is pretty current and well written. It's also helpful because it talks about the various offerings that Udemy has that represent ways you can then learn the skills. You can probably find similar articles at Coursera and Udacity (or ask their support team to point you to ones that show what courses can help you learn a particular skill).

The Data Science A-Z course uses Tableau

> In the article above they mention Tableau, and I think it's a good program to consider exploring, for a variety of reasons. When you are working with data it can be helpful to learn how to visualize it, to help people understand it. Tableau also happens to have a free version, and a well-developed ecosystem of projects and

hands-on examples to learn from, in order to "Try" data visualization.

Cars and other vehicles often have gears, even if you're automatically shifting, and I think Tableau for some people could be like a first gear to start in, as far as tools go. There's no wrong answer, but when you explore the field, you might simply start out by exploring Tableau – if you're working at a company it might also be an excellent way to connect with other people, especially if you're not in the "data" department.

1st Gear: Tableau
2nd Gear: R
3rd Gear: Python

For fun I put R as a possible second gear. There are some people who think R is easier to learn than Python. Maybe so. I still think Python is applicable enough outside of data science, which I'd recommend learning that first, but you might at least want to look at R at some point.

In the Udemy article, there's also some good information about the job market for data science:

> As more companies collect and analyze data, the field of data science remains a hot one. Glassdoor ranked "data scientist" as the top job of 2017, for the second year running. IBM predicts demand for data scientists will grow 28% by 2020. However, there is a shortage of data science talent as companies struggle to fill these new roles. McKinsey estimated the U.S. gap in data scientists would be around 140,000-190,000 by 2018, resulting in a demand that's 60% greater than supply.

--

What Are The Top Five Skills Data Scientists Need?

https://www.forbes.com/sites/quora/2017/06/15/what-are-the-top-five-skills-data-scientists-need/#707112ba7c0c

1. Programming
2. Quantitative analysis
3. Product intuition
4. Communication
5. Teamwork

> This is a good article that helps to understand some of the ways data science is used in business, and the importance of "soft" skills.
The Five Most In-Demand Skills For Data Analysis Jobs

https://www.forbes.com/sites/jeffkauflin/2017/07/20/the-five-most-in-demand-skills-for-data-analysis-jobs/#20e722cc2c7c

1. Data Analysis
2. SQL
3. Data Management
4. Business Intelligence
5. Data Warehousing

> This article is from the same publication, but shows a different perspective, and talks about some of the dynamics and systems in a business. If you think back to the diagram in a long ago chapter in this book, you can think of "data manufacturing", and learning how it flow through a business. In terms of SQL specifically, it can help you talk to a database, and would definitely help with the applied side of machine learning and data science, but might not be a pre-requisite for a machine learning course, per se. *I think it can also be helpful to consider that some of these skills may end up being best learned in the context of actually working at a business.*

--

9 Must-Have Skills You Need to Become a Data Scientist

https://www.kdnuggets.com/2014/11/9-must-have-skills-data-scientist.html

1. Education
2. SAS and/or R
2. Hadoop Platform
3. SQL Database/Coding
4. Python Coding
5. SQL Database/Coding
6. Unstructured data
7. Non-Technical: Intellectual Curiosity
8. Non-Technical: Business acumen
9. Non-Technical: Communication skills

I'm not sure there's necessarily nine – this might represent an example where some data science jobs may require some of the skills, or where the experience in those roles can help you to get the skills, but where a "machine learning engineer" may find themselves not necessarily using all of them. For example, even though data science and machine learning may be related, it may be that someone who gains python programming experience, along with knowledge of statistics, basic probability and linear algebra, could in theory get an internship or job as a machine learning engineer, without necessarily knowing SQL for example, SAS, the R programming language, or a big data platform like Hadoop.

> *Data scientists are highly educated – 88% have at least a Master's degree and 46% have PhDs – and while there are notable exceptions, a very strong educational background is usually required to develop the depth of knowledge necessary to be a data scientist.*

I think that his quote above is fair as well – some of the sophistication of the things we're talking about is often some combination of not only an undergraduate degree, with grounding in various fields that might include computer science or business, but possible a focused Master's Degree that is a step closer to the skills used in the workplace. Some people choose to go directly into a Master's Degree, others find it useful to launch out into the workplace, and learn more advanced parts of a field while working, so that you can get a good balance of theory and practice. There's not really any wrong answer.

But one thing I would say is that there are increasingly alternatives to traditional options for education. I myself believe that in person education is a good thing, including graduate degrees, but it's also true that there are people going through "coding bootcamps" who get programming jobs with 6 months of intensive work. And for someone who is working, part-time or full-time, a traditional degree is not the only option: not only are there free online courses, but there are non-traditional things like "nanodegrees" where you can work towards a certificate of some kind, with access to a mentor or instructor. And even with Master's degrees, case in point, Udacity has a special deal with AT+T to offer an online Master's Degree in computer science.

To simplify navigating the possibilities, depending on what your life stage is, I'd consider always keeping an eye out for actual work opportunities to learn the skills in context, and starting to explore in-person and online options for learning. Try them out, and talk to people who've done them; the most important thing may not be the exact channel that you learn from, but just getting going.

The only thing I'd say to people who would write themselves out of taking a PhD is the fact that I'm a good example of someone who never thought I'd be teaching: I'm the rock n roll guy who fell off a bus, remember? In the field of AI in particular, some of the most exciting work is being done by PhD's, professors and their grad students – people who were doing cutting-edge research at universities, and then all the big companies started battling to hire them. You don't have to have a PhD, but if you end up liking the theoretical side, or you read a book like Master Algorithm and your mind catches on fire, you might want to consider going for a PhD. The important thing about getting a PhD to note is that yes, you end up helping others to learn in some way, but there are people who focus on research, and there are others who focus on teaching, and either path is good.

In my own case, I simply found that at differing work situations, I found that I enjoyed helping other people to understand technical things, to learn things I had learned how to do. This workplace learning, and showing a friend how to do something, gradually grew into the idea of teaching. And I never, ever thought of myself "lecturing" in front of a class, but I started out more in a computer lab environment, basically doing the same thing I did at work: showing people how to do things, answering their questions, following up and helping people, and that helped me to see that I wanted to do it full-time. There's a desperate need and a lot of opportunity.

So I'd consider getting your feet wet, and then going as far and high as you want, whatever that means to you.

How companies are using big data and analytics

https://www.mckinsey.com/business-functions/mckinsey-analytics/our-insights/how-companies-are-using-big-data-and-analytics
> Another good article on how data science is being "applied"

How the Most Successful Companies Effectively Leverage Data and Analytics for Problem Solving

http://data-informed.com/how-the-most-successful-companies-effectively-leverage-data-and-analytics-for-problem-solving/
> Likewise. If artificial intelligence and machine learning is an extension of

data science, then at all levels, it's helpful to remember that leveraging them can help a business compete, and part of that competition comes from solving problems.

Accelerated Data Science

Part of the reason I'm pausing to raise the possibility of "accelerated" data science is to highlight the fact that platforms and tools for AI and machine learning, and data science, will all evolve. DataRobot is a good example of a tool at the intersection of these areas right now, where they are trying to make it easier to leverage AI without requiring the PhD. So learning more and trying some of the platforms can help, whether you are seeking a role, or advocating for a business to experiment with AI. (This also applies to non-profits – non-profits don't often have enough $$ to hire more highly-paid technical staff, but the DataRobot does have a case study of a business that helps non-profits, who is facing the talent shortage, and using AI to help non-profits.)

Machine Learning for Dummies?

There are a lot of options out there. If videos don't do it for you, if your eyes glaze over, if you have a headache, and if you may have a history of trying a Dummies book in the past, then it might be time to consider a Dummies book now.

If you fall into this category potentially, a prescription for you might be "this" 1-2-3 sequence:

1. Adapt: do read some articles each week; start with chapter 3 and then maybe explore the TechEmergence site. Maybe get the Time Magazine special edition on artificial intelligence to start. Lots of nice pictures, easy reading.
2. Adopt: try the DataRobot platform until or unless you get a headache. Keep trying. Try the platforms in small doses.
3. Adept: crack open the YouTube app and watch a few videos, and when you're for it, crack open DataCamp and explore Python, just to see what it's like. Research more about coal miners who are

becoming coders, and don't write yourself off. Order Machine Learning for Dummies and read it.

https://www.amazon.com/Machine-Learning-Dummies-John-Mueller/dp/1119245516

I think it's pretty great that there's a Machine Learning for Dummies book. I haven't read it, but I may very well do so. It looks like it is published "relatively" recently, and there's a pretty good chance that it may people who need a simpler path. Check it out, read through it, and by all means, make posts on Facebook for friends and family to see as you walk through it. Try making a blog, and share your thoughts, and take those blog posts and share them on Facebook or LinkedIn. The writing, the sharing, the discussion, will help.

https://www.amazon.com/Data-Science-Dummies-Lillian-Pierson/dp/1119327636

I also think it's great that there's a Data Science for Dummies book. Just like this book has room for improvement, I'm sure these Dummies books have room for improvement – it's not easy to try and face a field like AI and help people learn about it. One of the valuable things I'm sure those authors would appreciate, as much as I'd appreciate it – is feedback. Not from experts – but from *non-experts*: how did it come across? Was there something you didn't get? Questions you had? So if you read either Dummies book, I recommend trying to email the authors. And of course, I recommend you do the same with me – visit http://tsunami.ai/ and use the contact form. Feedback welcome!

Try a Path

We've covered a lot of territory in this chapter, and in some ways, it comes down to trying a path. It won't be the same for everyone, but let's review some of the options:

In-Person Class: In some ways, I think this is one of the best options for anyone to consider, if you have the time. You will be able to have some structure for you to help the learning keep ongoing, you'll have a mentor you can ask questions, and other students you can study with. Take a class, maybe it will lead to a certificate, maybe you'll end up wanting to take a degree. To me, in-person education is the best way to learn, the strongest way, all things considered.

Apps: to supplement other forms of learning, including the classroom, I think apps are a great way to go, including to help simplify the "Starting point" down to an app on your phone or tablet. You can learn quite a lot just from an app. At some point you'll need to start *trying* things, but an app like Datacamp can be a great way to start, including for developing the habit of learning. Just like keeping track of the news on AI, and trying platforms, building a habit of learning, taking actual courses, is important. In my opinion, anything that helps someone to start, and keep going, is good. Try an app!

Tools: for some people, trying a tool can be good. This might especially be the case if you're in a job already, and you learn enough to know that most people who are trying to do a particular thing, are using a tool such as _____.

149

Which tool depends on the level. A tool like Tableau, for data visualization, has a well developed ecosystem, with lots of learning material. Dive in! In terms of deep learning and machine learning, there are tools like Tensorflow from Google, and SageMaker from Amazon – where there will increasingly be books, courses, tutorials, oriented around the tool, which can help you learn a lot. I'd say, explore tools, read about them, make a list. If a particular tool catches your eye, explore it and don't worry about your experience level. If you find out that you need more background knowledge – go get it. One of the interesting ways to explore what kinds of tools are out there is to look at job descriptions. Try typing in "machine learning engineer" or "data scientist". Sometimes this technique can help confirm a sense you have the specific tools may be important to consider at some point.

Community: I do believe that in-person community is the best kind, when you can find it. For any given part of what you are seeking to learn, meetup.com can often lead you to a group of people who are seeking to learn the same thing, and there are often experts in the groups who can give you wisdom, tips, and potentially introductions for jobs. Take any given programming language (ex: Python), or tool (ex: Tensorflow), and there's most likely a meetup group. If there's not one in your area, it might be worth traveling to participate in. You might even want to *start* one.

The other kind of community can be found online – LinkedIn has a lot of discussion groups that are worth looking into around particular tools, skills, fields, and programming languages. There are any number of discussion forums and platforms – and it can be a great way to not only learn, but to have people to turn to when you get stuck, as you are learning, or as you start working. Ask around, find people who are doing the type of job you might eventually want to do (ex: on linkedin), and ask them what online communities and news sources they access.

Conclusion

Thanks for taking the time to make it this far in the book. We've reached a major milestone – exploring all three levels: adapt, adopt, adept. There's a lot there, and it's worth thinking about, and most importantly, acting on.

I think the next two chapters are also important, helpful, and worth reading. In Chapter 7, we'll look at People and Perspectives, and explore AI through looking at some of the key people who have been involved in AI, as well as the related concepts of deep learning, machine learning and neural networks.

Then, in Chapter 8, we'll revisit the concept of Next Steps, and look at some specific books and courses that you may want to consider.

Remember, the most important thing to begin is simply the habit of reading about AI in the news, to keep an eye on it, and to help you build up energy to take action. If that's all you ever did, it's a *good* thing. Start there.

Then, crack open and learn about how you can *adopt* AI. And once you've done that, once it is a habit, then move on and start the habit of becoming adept in AI.

Best wishes in taking good intentions and translating them into action!

Chapter 7 - Getting to Know AI: People and Perspectives

In this chapter, I want to invite you to consider how artificial intelligence is a community, made up of people. I think it's helpful to get to know some of the people in AI, to help give context to phrases like "deep learning" and "neural networks". I also think it's valid to learn about some of the core concepts in AI, from the people who created them and brought them forward.

We'll meet a few of the leaders in the AI field, take a look at some of the resources they have that can help you learn, and towards the end of the chapter, there are a few interviews with perspective from people who work in and write about the field.

Profile: Andrew Ng – Stanford, Coursera, Baidu, deeplearning.ai

Andrew Ng is an AI leader; he was based out of Stanford, and helped to launch the "MOOC" revolution (Massively Open Online Courses), through co-founding Coursera. His Stanford courses on machine learning continue to be popular and influential, and anyone can take them: see www.coursera.com

I would definitely recommend taking a look at this "main" site, and some of the resources there.

http://www.andrewng.org/

Andrew Ng is VP & Chief Scientist of Baidu; Co-Chairman and Co-Founder of Coursera; and an Adjunct Professor at Stanford University. In 2011 he led the development of Stanford University's main MOOC (Massive Open Online Courses) platform and also taught an online Machine Learning class that was offered to over 100,000 students, leading to the founding of Coursera.

One of the things that is interesting is how Andrew ended up at Baidu, which is like Google in China, but then recently came back to the U.S., particularly to work on helping developing training material to help more people learn about *deep learning,* the latest advanced technique for using neural networks to help analyze and process data. That more recent set of resources is available through www.deeplearning.ai

To get a sense of where Andrew Ng is at, you might want to see one of his most recent videos and presentations:

The State of Artificial Intelligence
https://www.youtube.com/watch?v=NKpuX_yzdYs

As you get to know more about AI, I think this particular article can be helpful for context:

A Primer of Deep Learning
https://www.forbes.com/sites/forbesagencycouncil/2017/12/18/a-primer-on-deep-learning/

Until recently, neural networks were considered a fairly unsuccessful branch of artificial intelligence. All of that changed when pioneers like Geoffrey Hinton and Andrew Ng managed to create amazingly good image recognition systems built on massive neural networks that had been trained with large amounts of internet data.

It gives a good concise explanation of the topics and terms. In the next chapter I recommend a book on machine learning; there are 100 different ways to learn about it, but just starting out, this article does a good job.

Machine learning basically involves training an algorithm. Instead of just feeding data into an algorithm, the algorithm is dynamic. The other thing this article points out, which I think is helpful, is that neural networks can learn from their mistakes.

So basically, the most recent advances in artificial intelligence have allowed data processing to go far beyond just processing data with a fixed formula: everything is dynamic, it's getting more sophisticated, and if you remember from earlier in the book, they are modeling things based on the way that the human brain works.

Profile: Geoffrey Hinton – University of Toronto, Google

https://en.wikipedia.org/wiki/Geoffrey_Hinton

> *Geoffrey Everest Hinton is a British cognitive psychologist and computer scientist, most noted for his work on artificial neural networks. As of 2015 he divides his time working for Google and University of Toronto. He was one of the first researchers who demonstrated the use of generalized backpropagation algorithm for training multi-layer neural nets and is an important figure in the deep learning community.*

Don't be alarmed at the vocabulary in the prior paragraph. Yup, it's a mouthful! Just remember that an algorithm is a tool for processing data, and the most recent advances attempt to mimic the way that the human brain works; and Geoffrey is responsible for some of the recent advances that have had such a tremendous impact. One of the ways to get a sense of how it all ties together is to read Master Algorithm.

Mini Interview

I didn't necessarily expect to hear back at all, but to make it easy, I tried asking Mr. Hinton a single question.

Todd: What inspired you originally to pursue artificial intelligence? What fuels your ongoing interest?

Geoffrey: I want to know how the brain works. I believe that the best way to understand it is to try to build one.

You may want to take a look at Geoffrey's academic homepage: http://www.cs.toronto.edu/~hinton/

I'd also recommend doing a couple YouTube searches.

(YouTube search: Geoffrey Hinton)

This interview is a fairly recent one, and gives some context for the impact of AI.

The Times Interviews Geoffrey Hinton, An A.I. Pioneer in Canada
https://www.youtube.com/watch?v=rtGXv88UQ-c
NY Times reporter Cade Metz interviews Geoffrey Hinton, professor emeritus of computer science at the University of Toronto who is a pioneer of A.I.

(YouTube search: Geoffrey E. Hinton (with the E))

This is another interview, which can give some additional context.

The Code That Runs Our Lives
https://www.youtube.com/watch?v=XG-dwZMc7Ng

> *From searching on Google to real-time translation, millions of people use deep learning every day, mostly without knowing it. It's a form of artificial*

intelligence designed to mimic the human brain. Geoffrey Hinton is a professor in the department of computer science at the University of Toronto. His work on deep learning has been snapped up by Google and is now being used to power its search engine. He joins The Agenda to discuss deep learning and the future of artificial intelligence.

Profile: Pedro Domingos – University of Washington, Master Algorithm

Pedro is not only the author of the excellent book Master Algorithm, but he also teaches at University of Washington. I'd suggest taking a look at his academic home page:

https://homes.cs.washington.edu/~pedrod/

There are several resources there worth filing away, including YouTube videos for his online machine learning class, and several TEDx talks that are worth checking out.

And I would definitely recommend reading Master Algorithm, whenever you are ready, to help get a better sense of how things came together for machine learning, the core concepts, and some of the opportunities.

One nice link from the academic home page is a special PDF file that is the Prologue of the book. Definitely worth reading.

https://homes.cs.washington.edu/~pedrod/Prologue.pdf

Fei Fei Li – Stanford, Google

Fei Fei Li is another example of a professor who is a leader in the field of AI; one of her specialties is "computer vision", such as using AI to help visual applications such as self-driving cars and image identification, etc.

http://vision.stanford.edu/feifeili/
Fei-Fei Li is an Associate Professor of Computer Science at US Stanford University. She is the director of the Stanford Artificial Intelligence Lab (SAIL) and the Stanford Vision Lab. She works in the areas of computer vision and cognitive neuroscience.

Her academic page is a bit sparse, relatively speaking, but if you haven't already, I'd recommend reading this article and the others mentioned in chapter 3, about how Google is moving into China.

Google opens Chinese AI lab, says 'science has no borders' https://www.theverge.com/2017/12/13/16771134/google-ai-lab-china-research-center

I would also recommend taking a look at some of the videos available on YouTube, by typing in her name, including these two specific ones:

Computer vision is a good example of a field where AI is having a significant impact. I also like the second video, in terms of how it celebrates startups, and the need for a diverse community to get involved, from organizations both large and small.

Interview: Jim Spohrer - IBM

James C. Spohrer is a computer scientist best known for having led the development of a new science of service systems, often known as service science, management and engineering. In spring 2017, Spohrer was named as Director, Cognitive OpenTech for IBM. From 2009 through 2016, he had been the Director of IBM Global University Programs Worldwide.

—

Interview

Q: Jim, what does your typical customer profile look like, if there is one?

All entities that use and/or contribute to "open AI code + data + models" (a type of resource) as part of a service they offer to others.

Q: How long do you think it will be before AI trickles down significantly from enterprise into medium and small business?

It already has, see Domingos "The Master Algorithm" - or just appreciate the fact when you do a Google search, look at a social media post, buy things from Amazon, consider an online recommendation, use an online map to get somewhere, you are benefitting from years of AI research on pattern recognition, machine learning, knowledge representation, and automated reasoning. See: https://www.amazon.com/Master-Algorithm-Ultimate-Learning-Machine/dp/0465065708

Q: How far do you think the current approaches in neural networks can take us before there is some kind of plateau?

Deep learning is a type of multilayer optimization that requires a lot of data and a lot of compute power. With enough data and enough compute power, pattern recognition models can be developed that are as good as individual people (typically 5% error rates) and in some cases super-human performance levels. The next challenge is episodic memory and commonsense reasoning - do we have enough data? do we have enough compute power? No, not yet. Are the current algorithms alone sufficient? Unlikely that they are, but there is a lot of investment to try to find out more. We will know more once we achieve petascale on data and algorithms at around $1000 cost - estimated by 2040. We are still at the terascale level (what $1000 buys),and petascale is 1000x terascale. The human brain is estimated at the exascale, and that is 1000x petascale. Exascale is estimated to be $1000 cost by 2060. For more see: http://service-science.info/archives/4741

Q: What would your advice be to college students heading towards the job market, in terms of choosing a career in light of what AI can accomplish?

Think about the service you can offer to others in society, based on your interests. Find others with your same interests, who have been succeeding in offering a service to others and learn as much as you can from them. Find and learn from many, many role models. Students should start thinking about making a job and not taking a job. In order to "think beyond taking a job or making career" requires understanding aspirations or even callings. First remember AI will make access to knowledge cheaper, and that is good thing for tackling unsolved challenges both technical and social. If you have a STEM (Science-Technology-Engineering-Math) leaning, learn to work on multidisciplinary teams to tackle unsolved problems. If you like working with STEM people, but are academically business-oriented, art-and-humanities oriented, or social sciences oriented, find a way to be helpful working on multidisciplinary teams to tackle unsolved problems - yours skills are needed to in many ways, from communications and marketing to making sure organizations of people run smoothly. At IBM we term, this type of person a T-shaped person, with problem-solving depth, and communication breadth. The world needs lots more T-shaped people.

When I mentor students, I ask them to come up with a good answer to the question - "What would you do if you have 100 workers working for you?" This prepares them for a future of digital workers based on AI, and how they want to augment themselves to offer service to others.

Q: What do you think would be the best path for someone who wants to break out of the gig economy into a more consistent ongoing full time position?

Same as above. Find others with your same interests, who are succeeding in offering service to others and learn as much as you can from them. To be the best, learn from the rest. Find role models, and get to know them.

Q: If a student or mid level career professional is open to reinventing themselves, what would be the skills and courses you would recommend that they take?

Find role models, and get to know them by helping them solve problems.

Q: In light of changes coming from workforce evolution; what advice would you have for colleges to evolve their curriculum? Ground every student in coding and AI, and develop familiarity with the functional areas of business without specializing?

Lean into entrepreneurship. Recruit entrepreneurial faculty. Recruit entrepreneurial students. Create a diverse startup ecosystem that is a thicker-and-thicker ring around your campus. See:

http://www.therepublic.com/2017/09/17/purdue_pushes_entrepreneurial_initiative/

If students are interested in coding and AI great. However, if they are not teach them to be T-shaped with depth and breath, and able to identify role models with related interests, and to help role models solve problems.

Q: Some people look at the trending and call for a tax on automation; others call for universal basic income, and others think it would be impossible to enforce. What's your view? Do you think we're headed in that direction, and do you think there is any justification for it?

Many experiments are best, since one size does not fit all. Taxing automation is just one way to fund a universal basic income, and there are others. I suggest people read this book: https://www.amazon.com/Accelerating-TechnOnomic-Medium-ATOM-Upgrade-ebook/dp/B072K3JL29

Q: AutoML seems to raise the stakes for what AI can accomplish - do you think it will be possible for startups to compete with larger players?

Yes, startups will do fine. The question I am asked more often is "will large companies survive?" Yes, both will do fine. Many good books out there on this, but I enjoyed this one most recently: https://www.amazon.com/Get-off-Grass-Kickstarting-Innovation-ebook/dp/B00GF2MOAQ/

Q: Have any movies or books influenced you in thinking about AI?

See books above. I liked the movie Her: https://en.wikipedia.org/wiki/Her_(film)

I also blog about a lot of books - see: http://service-science.info/archives/4416

Interview: AI and the Future of Work - a discussion with Irving Wladawsky-Berger

Irving Wladawsky-Berger is an expert in emerging technology, a regular contributor to the Wall Street Journal's CIO Journal, and a Visiting Lecturer at MIT's Sloan School of Management, as well as Adjunct Professor at the Imperial College Business School. He was born in Cuba and came to the US at the age of 15, and was named Hispanic Engineer of the Year in 2001. He has an M.S. and Ph. D. in physics from the University of Chicago. To learn more about Irving, see - http://www.irvingwb.com/ - on that site, you can subscribe with your email address to his blog.

The discussion below is in relation to a conference that took place at MIT with various AI professionals and researchers, and the question of the impact of AI on the job market. If you're interested in the question, "What's Going to Happen? And When?", I highly recommend reading the related blog post: http://blog.irvingwb.com/blog/2017/12/ai-and-the-future-of-work.html

--

Todd: Irving, I appreciated your blog post on AI and the future of work about the conference at MIT. It was really interesting to hear about that meeting, it feels like a watershed moment of some kind, especially with the people who were there. It has really come closest of anything I've seen so far, to providing solid evidence, perhaps the first I've seen that is convincing to me at least, of the potential for AI to have flat or eventual net job increase. I think this particular quote from one of the attendees was striking:

> *No invention in the 250 years since the first industrial revolution has caused mass unemployment, and that though jobs are constantly being destroyed, they are also being created in even larger numbers*

But in spite of the evidence and data discussed at the meeting, it still feels like something may be different, meaning AI could end up replacing more jobs than it adds, and not just assisting people, but replacing them. I think what comes to mind is just the extent to which jobs and industries are virtualized these days, making them potentially easier to replace, and much faster than in past industrial transformations. In relation to the quote above, I'm also not sure there has ever been an invention like digitization, which began as a tool and has now been at the core of so many industries, not just speeding them up but actually absorbing them. If the computer was at first a tool and then the Internet was at first a set of tools, then it seems that virtualization has been a novel phenomenon.

Irving: Many people think that this time is different, that our technologies, including virtualization, the Internet, AI, etc are different from anything we've seen in the past. But, many believe that the changes around the turn of the 20th century may have been even bigger, with electricity, indoor plumbing, cars, airplanes, telegraphs, radio, TV, etc. If you look at what life was like in advanced countries like the US, UK, etc in 1880 and compare it to what life was like in 1930 it was truly a gigantic difference, perhaps bigger than comparing today with life 50 years ago - 1967.

Todd: That seems worth taking into account. I did read the very recent McKinsey study that came out, and I recognize that it has fairly deep data, and suggests more of an optimist view. Like many other optimist sources, it recognizes there could be significant job lost, and I appreciate how it urges government leaders to make policy decisions in support of workforce transition. I want to believe its conclusion that in the end, based on the data they see, that more new jobs will be created, eventually, but I'm not quite convinced.

Irving: The MIT AI conference I wrote about in that blog post, and the McKinsey study discussed at the meeting, are some of the best explanations why we should be optimistic. There is no question that if managers can get the same work done with fewer people they will do so. But remember, new technologies and innovation will lead to new jobs and industries over time. So, as McKinsey said, there will be jobs lost, jobs transformed, and jobs gained, but in the end, McKinsey and most speakers at the AI conference felt that over time we'll be fine.

Todd: Ok, so if you can indulge me, please address the remaining doubt I have; let's say I want to be an optimist, but I keep thinking how in the business world and many other fields, so much of it is already digitized, which seems to argue that disruption could happen a lot quicker, and that it may be a reason why more jobs could be lost. If a great deal of jobs use digital tools, making it easier to automate them, then it seems possible. Even in the McKinsey report, with all due respect, they mostly seem to be doing predictive analysis based on past trends, and they don't seem to address the phenomena of how digitized work is. Maybe even more simply, it seems like if something can be automated, it will be, and because of digitization, it seems like the speed and scale could have a more significant impact on the past.

What do you think about the issue of digitization? Would you agree that in spite of the data in the McKinsey report and similar ones, that the impact of digitization may be a wildcard, which could potentially make this disruption more impactful? Do you think that the virtualization and automation of tasks could make the disruption from AI different than the inference and projection made by Mr Gordon?

Irving: Todd, let me try to address your very reasonable doubts based on research on the topic at MIT and McKinsey. The McKinsey study you referenced above explained that most occupations involve a number of activities, and just because some of the activities in a job have been automated, does not imply that the whole job has disappeared. Based on a detailed analysis of over 800 occupations, McKinsey concluded that less than 5 percent, consist of activities that can be entirely automated. However, in about 60 percent of all occupations, at least one-third of their constituent activities could be automated. This means that many more occupations will be significantly transformed than will be automated away by 2030.

Another piece of evidence comes from the MIT conference, where MIT professor Erik Brynjolfsson explained that AI is a general-purpose technology, like electricity, and such technologies require complementary innovations and investments that take quite a bit of time to play out before their benefits are felt across the economy and society. Realizing the benefits of AI, will probably require reinventing our organizations and institutions.

History suggests that eventually things work out, but there can be long, painful periods of transition.

Todd: Fair enough. I suppose I lean towards pessimism about net job loss, and if that is possible, it seems to have implications for individuals and policy makers that we could be in for some serious trouble. And if a greater danger is perceived, perhaps more people will wake up to it and take action. But I'm not an alarmist, because I see a lot of good coming from AI, and I can see the possibility of new jobs arising. But I guess we just don't know how big the impact will be and how fast.

Irving: We don't really know what the future will bring. There are techno-pessimists who think that there will be little innovation, mass unemployment, social disturbances, etc. There are techno-optimists who feel that we will once more adapt to technology advances just as we have for the past 250 years. I'm in the techno-optimist camp, but in the end, we don't really know.

Todd: The other part early in your article that I wanted to believe, that I *want* to believe, is the message I hear in various readings about the notion that only portions of jobs will be automated. It reminds me of the announcement earlier this year with big fanfare by Eric Schmidt, and a conference, that "90% of jobs are not fully automatable". But this feels more like wishful thinking, as opposed to grounded in corporate reality. It makes perfect sense if upper managements' priority was to protect full time jobs - but in a publicly traded company, I can hardly see a manager keeping 100% of full-time staff in situations where a significant portion of their tasks can be automated, especially if faced with economic uncertainty, declining revenues, or simply the constant need to increase profit. It seems more likely that they would reduce headcount.

If a CEO has the ethical shield of duty to shareholders, why would they not do what is best for the shareholders, which would be to be as profitable as possible, which would be to reduce waste as much as possible, and therefore automate as much as possible?

Irving: Todd, clearly companies will do what they have to, to increase productivity, revenue and profits, including as much automation as is feasible. But, as I mentioned earlier, the prediction that over 90% of jobs are not fully automatable in the next 15 to 20 years, is based on research at McKinsey, MIT and other universities and think tanks. The longer we have to adapt to AI and other transformative technologies, the more time we have to create new jobs and industries. But, remember that the fact that things work out over the long term does not mean that there isn't considerable pain in the short term, as many workers who don't have the skills to keep up with technology will be left behind. Being a techno-optimist does not mean that we shouldn't acknowledge that the transition will not be easy for many workers.

Todd: I guess the most important thing is not the question of whether there is net job loss or net job gain, but how do we respond, as societies and individuals. I'm guessing it would benefit government leaders to take a close look at your blog post, at the McKinsey report and other similar ones from Oxford, PwC, etc., as well as the work of Dr. Carlota Perez, mentioned at the meeting, which seems to strike a good balance and strongly recommend investment in infrastructure and renewable energy as one of the areas of job gain. The consensus them on a macro level seems to be that the more passive we are as individuals and societies, the negative impact of AI will be much greater. And conversely, we have a choice – the more active we are as individuals and societies in responding to AI, the better.

Irving: Precisely. Governments, business and individuals have a responsibility to do everything possible to adjust to this changing future, so that technology advances benefit everyone. As the Mckinsey report said in conclusion:

"Automation represents both hope and challenge. The global economy needs the boost to productivity and growth that it will bring, especially at a time when aging populations are acting as a drag on GDP growth. Machines can take on work that is routine, dangerous, or dirty, and may allow us all to use our intrinsically human talents more fully. But to capture these benefits, societies will need to prepare for complex workforce transitions ahead. For policy makers, business leaders, and individual workers the world over, the task at hand is to prepare for a more automated future by emphasizing new skills, scaling up training, especially for midcareer workers, and ensuring robust economic growth."

Conclusion

As you learn more about AI, I encourager you to look for more information about people in the AI community: their story, videos they may have made, interviews, books, etc. Your list might include "leaders", but it can also be helpful to get to know more about people who are involved at every level, including engineers, people who work at startups, or people who are using AI in business and science.

As much as I think that books and articles and courses are good ways to learn, I also think that in-person contact is great, especially for inspiration: you may want to consider exploring meetup.com for AI-related groups in your area (ex: machine learning, data science, artificial intelligence), as well as keeping your eyes open for events, such as conferences or conventions, where you can meet people who are working in the field.

As far as I know, even though the people in this chapter are considered leaders, they all agree how important it is to get more people involved. I think it's also helpful to consider a concept you sometimes hear in the field of programming, where because the demand is so great, yes there are positions and roles for being a software engineer, but there are also plenty of opportunities for people to apply expertise at other levels. For example, there are electrical *engineers*, who might design circuits or systems, but then there are also a lot of *electricians* out there, who might work on your apartment or house. I think it's especially appropriate to consider this when you have people like Andrew Ng claiming that AI is the new electricity (see his video on the topic). I do think the comparison is helpful, including the fact that you don't necessarily have to be an AI "engineer", you could be an AI "electrician" – still important, still valid, and maybe for some, a starting point.

In the next and last chapter, we'll look at a summary of some options for next steps.

Chapter 8: What to Do Next

In this chapter we'll take a look at a couple options for where to learn more. To keep the journey sustainable and to help with motivation, it's important to build the habits of keeping track of the news (adapt), and exploring platforms (adopt). This is partly because things can change fast in both areas. Then as soon as you're ready to become more adept, I'd recommend starting to read books and take at least one course.

The way this book is designed is to be an introduction and a simple reference you can come back to; in the case of what to do next, I'd say – keep re-reading chapters 3-6 until they are burned into your synapses. Chapter 6 has some good information on options for learning that you can turn to, we'll look at some new books to go beyond getting your feet wet, and several options for courses.

Try Each Format: the general advice I have when learning is to try each format. Read books, try a course locally, try online, see what works for you.

Books

Context is important; if you haven't already I'd recommend starting with *Rise of the Robots*, and *Master Algorithm*, as well as *2nd Machine Age* (and/or *Machine Platform Crowd*), to get a better sense of what the field is, the impact and importance, and how important it is.

Then, to take a step in the direction of becoming more adept in AI, I'd recommend the following two books:

Machine Learning

MIT has a nice series called Essential Learning – this introduction to Machine Learning is concise, and the format itself is approachable; the printed book is a bit smaller, easy to carry. I think it's a good starting point, it can help you understand some of the concepts, and to see how some of the pieces fit together, including ones you may need to learn.

https://www.amazon.com/Machine-Learning-Press-Essential-Knowledge/dp/0262529513

Deep Learning

When you make it through the Machine Learning book, in addition to reading articles, watching videos, I'd recommend investing in this book, to become gradually more familiar with the forefront of artificial intelligence. You don't have to be an expert in anything to read it – it's a bit like the Master Algorithm and the Machine Learning book – it can help you get a sense of the field.

I'd recommend reading it the same way I'd recommend reading Master Algorithm – don't worry if you don't necessarily "get" everything in the first reading. Skim through it if you need to, and come back to it again after you've taken a few courses.

https://www.amazon.com/Deep-Learning-Adaptive-Computation-Machine-ebook/dp/B01MRVFGX4

For what it's worth, it has a good review from Elon Musk:

> *"Written by three experts in the field, Deep Learning is the only comprehensive book on the subject. It provides much-needed broad perspective and mathematical preliminaries for software engineers and students entering the field, and serves as a reference for authorities."*

> - Elon Musk, co-chair of OpenAI; cofounder and CEO of Tesla and SpaceX

Courses

Ultimately I think that actual courses are probably the best way for just about anyone to develop expertise in artificial intelligence. Some may be able to get by with articles and books, but I think the structure is valuable, especially if you can afford the time to take a course where you are in community with others and have access to a mentor. I think that courses are probably one of the most sustainable ways to learn artificial intelligence, all things considered. AI is not "easy", but the framework of a course, in community, can help sustain and reinforce learning.

Go Local

I do believe that seeking out any local options at a community college or university or "bootcamp" could be one of the best ways to learn, because of the direct access to a mentor. Not easy, certainly, especially if you're working, but in terms of structure and mentors, and in person reinforcement, I think it's the best way to go.

You might be lucky and your area options might include certificates, programs or even degrees that are sequenced to help you get the right skills and knowledge. I wouldn't count on it though, which is why learning about some of the skills you might need can be helpful – it may be helpful to review some of the cutting edge online course programs, even just to see what skills and topics they cover, as well as the pre-requisites, and then see what you could learn locally. For some, that might be an introduction to data science or artificial intelligence – or it could be a math course.

Online/Book Refreshers

Remember that for some areas, if you need to brush up on statistics, algebra, or basic probability there may be books to help you, or even apps, such as Khan Academy, or DataCamp. You can find out some of the skills from looking at previous chapters, but you may also want to do what I did – enroll for the Machine Learning course from Stanford on Coursera (free if you use audit mode), get your feet wet, and look at the pre-requisites.

If you have experience with Excel, or you like the idea of learning with a program, there are books out there that can help you, with titles like "Statistics with Excel". For some that might be a good starting point. If you need all of the above as a refresher, some courses will cover those, and if you're not sure where to get started, start with basic statistics.

Coursera

In addition to individual courses, several providers have collections of courses, where you can earn a certificate, or in the case of Udacity, a "nanodegree". Some courses may be free and have an audit mode, others are paid. If you search long enough, these days you can probably find just about anything for free, but relative to the quality and "cohesiveness" of a set of courses, I'd recommend looking at Coursera and Udacity, and considering starting with a set of courses in data science or programming.

In Coursera, these are the top "specializations" – deep learning may be too advanced, but I'd look seriously at Python for Everybody (programming), Data Science, and Applied Data Science with Python. For example, you might want to start a free trial and take Python for Everybody.

Top Specializations

deeplearning.ai	University of Michigan	Johns Hopkins University	University of Michigan
Deep Learning	Python for Everybody	Data Science	Applied Data Science with Python
5 courses	5 courses	10 courses	5 courses

Paid and Audit Options

Be aware that some courses/specializations have various options for payment and auditing for free. When you click Enroll, there may or may not be a free audit option.

7-day Free Trial

✓ **Unlimited access to all courses in the Specialization**
Watch lectures, try assignments, participate in discussion forums, and more.

✓ **Cancel anytime.**
No penalties - simply cancel before the trial ends if it's not right for you.

✓ **$49 USD per month to continue learning after trial ends.**
Go as fast as you can - the faster you go, the more you save.

✓ **Certificate when you complete and after trial ends.**
Share on your resume, LinkedIn, and CV.

Start Free Trial

If you look at Coursera, I'd also definitely recommend looking in the Help section and reading this entire article on Enrollment options:

https://learner.coursera.help/hc/en-us/articles/209818613-Enrollment-options

It includes information on free vs paid., etc

When you audit a course:

- You'll be able to see most of the course materials for free, but you won't be able to submit certain assignments or get grades for your work.
- You won't be able to submit assignments for feedback or a grade.
- You won't get a Course Certificate.

To audit a course:

- Open the home page of the course you want to audit
- Click **Enroll**
- At the bottom of the window, click **audit** or choose the "Audit only" option

There's no wrong answer, but if you can afford it, I'd recommend considering using the paid version and working towards an actual certificate, both to help give you a sense of accomplishment, and also to put on your resume and LinkedIn profile. Note: Coursera, and Udacity both have apps, so you can learn from your phone or tablet if you like.

Master's Degree via Coursera

In addition to looking at local programs, you might want to consider one of Coursera's new online Master's Degree programs in Computer Science, with a focus on data science and other core areas. A Master's Degree isn't required to get a job, but in general, they will pay for themselves over time, especially in a field where there is strong demand. Getting an in-person or online Master's Degree could be a good option, and some employers might pay for it.

Master of Computer Science in Data Science

Degree by University of Illinois

Builds expertise in four core areas of computer science: data visualization, machine learning, data mining and cloud computing.

25 courses | 15 - 20 hours per week   Learn More
18 - 36 months

The cost of this particular Master's Degree is relatively less than some, and it takes a commitment, but if you're ready to make one, it might be worth looking at, including if you need to get financial aid.

AT A GLANCE

12-36 months

8 16-week courses

$19,200 plus fees

Completely online

Udacity

There are more options out there than Coursera and Udacity, but I think they are pretty good examples. On Udacity, I'd recommend considering their "Learn to Code" nanodegree. If you try Udacity and like it, you might want to start with the Learn to Code nanodegree, and then go on to the Data Foundations and Data Analyst nanodegree.

Learn to Code

https://www.udacity.com/course/intro-to-programming-nanodegree--nd000

NANODEGREE PROGRAM

Learn to Code

Udacity's Intro to Programming is your first step towards careers in Web and App Development, Machine Learning, Data Science, AI, and more! This program is perfect for beginners.

> I like how the Learn to Code nanodegree starts with HTML, and moves from there to python. HTML is the basic language for making web pages, is relatively easy to learn, and it can help as a way to start coding.

Data Foundations

https://www.udacity.com/course/data-foundations-nanodegree--nd100

> I like how the Data Foundations nanodegree uses common and familiar tools as a way to help people get started in data science. Remember the top skills for data scientists? Go back and read a few of those articles in chapter 6, and come back here and take another look. Among other things, Tableau is a great tool for learning data visualization.

Data Analyst

https://www.udacity.com/course/data-analyst-nanodegree--nd002

I think this nanodegree would be a natural step after the previous two, and help to make a good foundation for machine learning, giving the programming and data skills to make it realistic. Udacity also has nanodegrees that are more advanced, in machine learning and artificial intelligence. And you may want to consider taking Andrew Ng's Coursera track in Machine Learning, or the deeplearning.ai courses, after getting a foundation, wherever you get it from. (And it might help to at least look at the advanced stuff, to get a sense of how the foundational skills fit it).

Master's Degree

Udacity has an interesting Master's Degree, that may be one of the least expensive yet "legit" online master's degrees in computer science, connected to Georgia Tech. You can also take some of the courses for free. It's a bit more general than a specific nanodegree, but may be good for some people.

https://www.udacity.com/georgia-tech

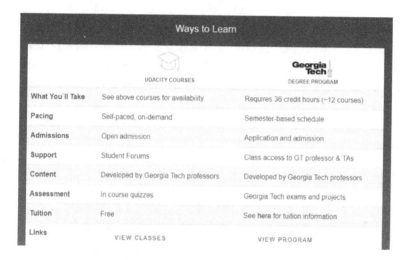

Ways to Learn		
	UDACITY COURSES	Georgia Tech DEGREE PROGRAM
What You'll Take	See above courses for availability	Requires 36 credit hours (~12 courses)
Pacing	Self-paced, on-demand	Semester-based schedule
Admissions	Open admission	Application and admission
Support	Student Forums	Class access to GT professor & TAs
Content	Developed by Georgia Tech professors	Developed by Georgia Tech professors
Assessment	In course quizzes	Georgia Tech exams and projects
Tuition	Free	See here for tuition information
Links	VIEW CLASSES	VIEW PROGRAM

The Georgia Tech page is also worth looking at for the program.
http://www.omscs.gatech.edu/

At the time of writing, the entire Master's Degree program is only $7,000 USD, and there may be options for paying over time, "as you go", as well as for financial aid.

AI Certification

This section is more wishful thinking than fact – at the current time, there aren't really many options for a certification in AI, or really "any" established options, based on a simple google search. But I think it's worth doing, in case something comes up.

Do you know of an AI certification? Are you interested in helping to develop one? Are you interested in getting one? If any of these are true please visit http://tsunami.ai and let me know.

It reminds me a bit of search engine optimization. Some fields have a lot of certifications, which are professional credentials that can help with employment by certifying that you have the right skills. In digital marketing, there are established certifications for some areas, such as Google Adwords and Google Analytics, but there really isn't an established, widely recognized SEO certification – just a number of smaller independent companies offering their own certifications.

Things may change at any time, but the only certification a search came up with seemed relatively new, less than $1,000 USD, but the certification itself doesn't seem industry recognized.

http://www.zarantech.com/ai-machine-learning-training/

But there certainly is market potential, and I think there's a strong need:

https://www.businesswire.com/news/home/20170922005032/en/Artificial-Intelligence-Certification-Courses---Market-Drivers

So if you're interested, or know of one, please let me know.

The best thing at present is probably to get a nanodegree or a "certificate", which shows having completed particular courses. A certification is generally more involved, where specific industry knowledge is tested. A certification is not as good as experience, but it can help you get noticed by recruiters and to get a job, and certifications can also be a good way for an industry to help develop talent. My guess is that the talent shortage is so severe, and people are so busy, that there aren't really any options out there. There are probably some companies and organizations working on something, hopefully.

Conclusion

Wowee – we've reached the end of the book! This is the end of the book, but not of our learning journey. I hope that you've found this book helpful to introduce concepts and provide some suggested resources for further learning.

Best wishes on your learning journey, and on surfing the tsunami!

-Todd

P.S. I would greatly, greatly appreciate if you could visit http://tsunami.ai and let me know any feedback you might have, good bad or indifferent. Even a single sentence would help – was there something you particularly appreciated, or that got your attention? Were you confused? Excited? Was there something missing? Was there anything you felt was distracting, unclear, or inappropriate? Please let me know.

Appendix A: 2019 Update

This is the complete set of data and articles gathered throughout 2018 and into 2019, for the 2019 edition. The categories include evidence of impact on jobs, interesting advances, opposing viewpoints, etc. If you are reading the print edition, and want clickable links, etc., see:
http://tsunami.ai/2019

Disclaimer: the pace of AI advances is so fast, I kept gathering material and pushing back the publication date of the 2019 edition; I finally decided to make it an appendix in the print edition. If you haven't read the earlier part of the book you may want to start there. My apologies for this appendix being a bit rough around the edges; I had decided it would be better to release than to wait until it is perfect. Feel free to email me feedback or questions at tekelsey@gmail.com - and please feel free to connect with me on LinkedIn: http://linkedin.com/in/tekelsey

AI in Five Minutes: 2018-2019 Milestones

I think this year's theme could be: AI Affects Everyone.

If you had only five minutes to glance through this, these are some of the things that stuck out to me since writing the first edition of Surfing the Tsunami.

1. **MIT** announces Interdisciplinary AI College

   The President of MIT's official release calling on education and government to support AI, as well as interdisciplinary AI education, to help people become "AI Bilingual":
   http://news.mit.edu/2019/president-reif-oped-federal-opportunity-and-threat-ai-0211

   Why This Is Important: because major institutions are starting to not only see the importance of AI, but to also see how it's not just a matter for computer scientists - MIT is seeking to help students in every discipline to learn how to leverage AI. I believe their goal is supported by the data I've seen, and that this has implications for individuals and educational institutions.

2.   **Google/Amazon** release all their internal training material on machine learning for the public.

Learn from ML experts at Google
https://ai.google/education/
Whether you're just learning to code or you're a seasoned machine learning practitioner, you'll find information and exercises to help you develop your skills and advance your projects.

> Amazon's own 'Machine Learning University' now available to all developers
> https://aws.amazon.com/blogs/machine-learning/amazons-own-machine-learning-university-now-available-to-all-developers/
> https://aws.amazon.com/training/learning-paths/machine-learning/
> (includes paths for business decision makers)
> Plus certification: aws.training/machinelearning

> Why This Is Important: Not only are these great resources for learners and educators, but it shows how the need for AI resources for "all" people is becoming increasingly important.

3.   **Kai Fu Lee** challenges individuals, educators and governments to face AI.

Facial and emotional recognition; how one man is advancing artificial intelligence
(Video - 60 Minutes - 1.13.19)
https://www.cbsnews.com/news/60-minutes-ai-facial-and-emotional-recognition-how-one-man-is-advancing-artificial-intelligence/
Scott Pelley reports on the developments in artificial intelligence brought about by venture capitalist Kai-Fu Lee's investments and China's effort to dominate the AI field.

Why This Is Important: Kai Fu Lee is an AI expert with valuable insight from working in both the United States and China - and he is kind; he cares.

4.   **Joseph Aoun**, President of Northeastern University, calls for lifelong learning, in light of AI

When it comes to lifelong learning, are universities the providers of last resort?
https://www.linkedin.com/pulse/when-comes-lifelong-learning-universities-providers-last-joseph-aoun/

"It is no longer debatable that artificial intelligence will transform our economy; the only question is the precise size of the tsunami. Numerous studies predict that up to 50 percent of today's jobs will disappear over the next two decades. In developing economies it could be up to 70 percent."

> A good article that talks about the implications of AI on the job market as well as the need for lifelong learning for those who either never had college or graduated from college.
> And he even used the word tsunami!

Why This Is Important: more solid evidence of the need for people of all ages to learn more, and for educators to develop life-long strategies.

5.   **Individuals** and educators take action (This means you, and me)
You: This means you. You're reading this; you're taking action. Our time is precious because it is finite. But I think this issue is worth investing time in. I encourage you to invest in your future, the future of your family, and country, by setting aside time to read the entire book, and other books (like Master Algorithm, especially) and every article I mention, and start learning more. Just by starting to read, you're at the Adapt stage - you're adapting to AI. I invite you to start moving towards Adopt - learn about the platforms. And in the Learn AI section, you can take steps to become more adept in AI. (What? Adapt/Adopt/Adept? See the Introduction)

Me: Here's my reaction to the announcement from Rafael Reif that calls for interdisciplinary action and education:

Helping Students to Become AI Bilingual - with Personal Data
https://www.linkedin.com/pulse/helping-students-become-ai-bilingual-personal-data-todd-kelsey/

Why This Is Important: We all need to find ways of helping each other to face AI, for the sake of our careers, our families and countries. On the note of families, the article above is an epiphany I had, realizing that personal data and life stories might be a meaningful way to help people learn more about data, from the vantage point of their own life stories and the ancestry and heritage of their family and community.

For more information about Rafael Reif of MIT, Joseph Aoun, and Kai Fu Lee see the "Learn from Leaders" section for more information and perspective from

Learn from Leaders

I'm highlighting what I think is some of the most important, relevant and insightful coverage on AI in 2018 and 2019, from several leaders who have important perspective on AI. Their perspective has helped inspire me to learn more myself as well as to get the 2019 edition of the book done so I could share it with you.

Rafael Reif, President of MIT

Fact: MIT is developing a new AI college, and seeking to help students in *every discipline* to increase their technical skills and to leverage AI

Implication: you don't have to be MIT to come to the same conclusion, and personally I think collaboration is necessary between schools, all their departments, companies and governments around the world to help students in any school to learn more, as well as anyone, of any age, who is not currently in school. That's the main reason I wrote this book.

The President of MIT's official release calling on education and government to support AI, as well as interdisciplinary AI education.
http://news.mit.edu/2019/president-reif-oped-federal-opportunity-and-threat-ai-0211

A related opinion piece he wrote discussing AI bilinguality:
https://www.ft.com/content/24f18c28-2a39-11e9-9222-7024d72222bc

A nice video clip from Switzerland (brrr!) with the same message:
http://news.mit.edu/news-clip/clip-wsj-large-artificial-intelligence-will-be-part-college-curriculum-mit-president

Joseph Aoun, President of Northeastern University

With Changing Students and Times, Colleges Are Going Back to School
https://mobile.nytimes.com/2018/04/05/education/learning/colleges-adapt-changing-students.html

(Comment from Todd: The kind of information pointed to by the excerpt below leads me to believe that facing this issue is an urgent question; the bolded statement (my bold) seems to additional confirmation that this is a *now* issue, not a future issue.)

> *That keeps Joseph E. Aoun, president of Northeastern University in Boston, up at night. While other presidents in local college towns worry about competing for endowments and enrollment, Mr. Aoun sees another threat: robots.*
>
> *More than the latest polls, he is driven by a 2013 Oxford University Study that predicted that nearly half of the jobs in the United States are at risk of being taken over by computers within the next two decades. "We said if robots are going to replace human beings we need to help students to be robot-proof, and we built a strategic plan around that," Mr. Aoun said.*
>
> *That thinking positioned Mr. Aoun on the fringe of higher education strategizing just a few years ago, **but he is now called on weekly to advise other institutions on how to help their students outsmart the workers of the future.***

--

When it comes to lifelong learning, are universities the providers of last resort?
https://www.linkedin.com/pulse/when-comes-lifelong-learning-universities-providers-last-joseph-aoun/
> A good article that talks about the implications of AI on the job market as well as the need for lifelong learning for those who either never had college or graduated from college.
He even used the word tsunami!

--

> *It is no longer debatable that artificial intelligence will transform our economy; the only question is the precise size of the tsunami. Numerous studies predict that up to 50 percent of today's jobs will disappear over the next two decades. In developing economies it could be up to 70 percent.*

> *These same forces will create new jobs that we can't even dream of today. But those jobs alone will not be sufficient: Just one in 10 workers are currently employed in fields that are projected to grow. Additionally, more than one in three existing jobs will require entirely different skill sets in the future.*

--

Joseph also has a good book that may be of interest to those in higher education.

(There's even an audiobook version - woohoo!
https://www.amazon.com/gp/aw/d/0262535971/ref=tmm_pap_tit
le_0)

Kai Fu Lee, Expert on AI in U.S., China

Kai Fu Lee is an AI expert and venture capitalist who has concrete advice
and perspective about AI and its impact on jobs, as well as the important of
AI education, and the need for government support. He is a leader in China

but spent many years in the U.S. and has gone out of his way to challenge all governments to face AI (including supporting education and facing the impact of job displacement).

CBS 60 Minutes: Facial and emotional recognition; how one man is advancing artificial intelligence
(Video - 1.13.19)
https://www.cbsnews.com/news/60-minutes-ai-facial-and-emotional-recognition-how-one-man-is-advancing-artificial-intelligence/
Scott Pelley reports on the developments in artificial intelligence brought about by venture capitalist Kai-Fu Lee's investments and China's effort to dominate the AI field

How to Prepare for AI Job Displacement
https://www.linkedin.com/pulse/how-prepare-ai-job-displacement-kai-fu-lee/

- *As individuals, we should accept that routine jobs are going away. For young people in these routine jobs, start now by finding careers that fit your strengths and that are not easily replaced by AI. For older people, when early retirement is offered to you, consider accepting, with gig economy and volunteering to make some income and live a life you enjoy.*
- *We should encourage more people to go into service careers, choosing jobs into which they can pour their hearts and souls, spreading their love and experiences.*
- *We should embrace AI tools, especially for professionals, understanding that they will get better with more data and use. We should use these tools to do parts of our jobs, allowing them to do more of our routine tasks, freeing us to move into areas that are more suitable for humans.*

The Human Promise of the AI Revolution
Artificial intelligence will radically disrupt the world of work, but the right policy choices can make it a force for a more compassionate social contract.
https://www.wsj.com/articles/the-human-promise-of-the-ai-revolution-1536935115?mod=mhp

The new technology will wipe out a huge portion of work as we've known it, dramatically widening the wealth gap and posing a challenge to the human dignity of us all.

This unprecedented disruption requires no new scientific breakthroughs in AI, just the application of existing technology to new problems. It will hit many white-collar professionals just as hard as it hits blue-collar factory workers.

———

According to a June 2017 study by the consulting firm PwC, AI's advance will generate $15.7 trillion in additional wealth for the world by 2030. This is great news for those with access to large amounts of capital and data. It's very bad news for anyone who earns their living doing soon-to-be-replaced jobs.

———

The jobs that will remain relatively insulated from AI fall on opposite ends of the income spectrum. CEOs, home care nurses, attorneys and hairstylists are all in "safe" professions, but the people in some of these professions will be swimming in the riches of the AI revolution while others compete against a vast pool of desperate fellow workers.

———

BIO

Kai-Fu Lee is a Chinese venture capitalist, technology executive, writer, and an artificial intelligence (AI) expert. He is currently based in Beijing, China. In his book, published in 2018, AI Superpowers: China, Silicon Valley, and the New World Order Lee described how China was rapidly moving forward to become the global leader in AI, and may well surpass the United States, because of China's demographics and its amassing of huge data sets.

In a 28 September 2018 interview on the PBS Amanpour program, he emphasized that AI, with all its capabilities, will never be capable of creativity or empathy.
https://en.wikipedia.org/wiki/Kai-Fu_Lee

Kai's New Book: AI Superpowers

I think Kai Fu Lee's book is worth reading, to learn more about how AI works, the related issues, and opportunities for the future for individuals and countries. In the presentation I attended in Chicago in September of 2019, Kai explained that the publisher pushed for the stark national imagery on the cover. But as a person Kai Fu Lee is mild-mannered, and his perspective is very valuable. The book does touch on international themes - but the conclusions are not really "us vs them" - one of the most interesting conclusions is the interesting idea that governments can and should encourage the development of jobs requiring compassion and empathy. (See the CBS 60 Minutes video mentioned above)

https://www.amazon.com/AI-Superpowers-China-Silicon-Valley/dp/0358105587

Note: it's the #1 release in Government Management, and #1 in other categories.

My Thoughts: Kai Fu Lee is cool. I like how he is a superhero venture capitalist in China, but also had deep experience in the USA - but through life experience he is also compassionate, and calls on governments to support education, and the creation of jobs which AI may not be able to overcome (which to him, astonishingly and interestingly, means jobs involving compassion and love - he already assumes and cites evidence showing how AI will take many, many jobs away, even as it creates others)

I had the chance to meet Kai Fu Lee in September of 2018, and I had just read a good blog article that talked about a delineation emerging in data science jobs of data analyst, data scientist, and data engineers. Data analysts probably analyze, report, maybe visualize data. Data scientists work more deeply with the technical tools, and manage things like machine learning, neural networks and deep learning. Data Engineers would be the people who learn how data works, where it resides in companies, how to connect the systems, and the vast amount of work that goes into preparing data in order for AI and machine learning to be able to work with it.

So in the presentation he gave, which was on his book AI Superpowers (see bio below), I asked him, if we consider that AI has increasing powers to automate just about anything, what about automation of AI jobs themselves? I realized and proposed that maybe data engineers might have the most job security long term, because aspects of data analysis and data science might be easier to automate (not easy, but as AI increases in sophistication, witnessed even in the present by things like Google's AutoML, which was driven by the AI talent shortage to become an attempt to have AI create and manage itself, reducing the need for human input).

Kai agreed that data engineering might be the most secure, and maybe where the most positions will be. (For those interested in Enterprise AI and data engineering, see http://tsunami.ai/white-papers and look for the data integration paper from Amazon.)

Kai was kind enough to let me take a picture; and also kind enough to do an interview for the 2019 edition of Surfing the Tsunami.

My Favorite Article of 2018-2019

One of the main reasons I wrote this book is because I became convinced over time to take AI very seriously, and to explore the data to see both the opportunities and disruption of AI. To me the data points to more jobs being lost than created, but it is a complex issue and estimates do vary. To me, the very fact that advances in AI are so unpredictable, is one of the top reasons why I am skeptical about any claim that there will be more jobs created. The next reason is because it seems that so much of work is already digital; that advances in AI could automate work significantly faster than jobs can be created. My response has been to try and help people learn as much as possible, and to think about methods of creating jobs with AI.

This past year, I came across a third reason. In the following article, they talk about how 90% of the work in AI is working with data preparation (which bodes well for data engineers). So I might call this data inertia, the barriers to AI implementation. And on the surface it would seem like this is evidence of AI "slowing down", or less chance of it taking jobs.

Net Job Loss/debate - #1 article - 90% rule

When Genpact, an IT services company, helps businesses launch what they consider AI projects, "10% of the work is AI," says Sanjay Srivastava, the chief digital officer. "Ninety percent of the work is actually data extraction, cleansing, normalizing, wrangling."
—
https://www.technologyreview.com/s/612897/this-is-why-ai-has-yet-to-reshape-most-businesses/

Inspiration: Applications of AI

Finance

How machine learning and data science give Bloomberg a competitive advantage (Video, article)
https://www.zdnet.com/article/how-machine-learning-and-data-science-give-bloomberg-a-competitive-advantage/
CTO Shawn Edwards says strong AI capability helps the firm build data-led products for its customers.
> This also is an example of how AI = data science = machine learning

Business Intelligence in Finance – Current Applications (Updated 2.19)
https://www.techemergence.com/business-intelligence-in-finance-current-applications/
Reuters referenced a Stratistics MRC figure estimating the size of the business intelligence industry around $15.64 billion in 2016. It follows that AI would find its way into the business intelligence world. In our previous report, we covered 6 use-cases for AI in business intelligence. As of now, numerous companies claim to assist business leaders in the finance domain, specifically, in aspects of their roles using AI. We researched the space to better understand where AI comes into play in business intelligence in the finance industry and to answer the following questions
> Tools mentioned include RapidMiner, DataRobot, Domo
> TechEmergence, now Emerj, has a lot of good resources on the emerging AI industry and resources for connecting with it.

Wall Street Tech Spree: With Kensho Acquisition S&P Global Makes Largest A.I. Deal In History
https://www.forbes.com/sites/antoinegara/2018/03/06/wall-street-tech-spree-with-kensho-acquisition-sp-global-makes-largest-a-i-deal-in-history/
Nadler's initial plan for Kensho: Use machine learning to make complex financial analysis as easy as a search on Google.

Small Business

https://www.techemergence.com/how-machine-learning-will-become-accessible-to-small-businesses/

Real Estate

https://www.wsj.com/articles/how-to-buy-a-house-the-wall-street-way-1537102800?mod=mhp
> an article about how AI was applied in the real estate sector, for competitive advantage

Marketing

Assessing the Intelligence of AI Marketing Tech (2.19)
https://www.business2community.com/business-innovation/assessing-the-intelligence-of-ai-marketing-tech-02169399

General

7 popular AI use cases today
https://searchenterpriseai.techtarget.com/photostory/252453549/7-popular-AI-use-cases-today/1/Examples-of-AI-abound

Implementing AI

Data Management Experts Share Best Practices for Machine Learning (2.19)
http://www.dbta.com/Editorial/News-Flashes/Data-Management-Experts-Share-Best-Practices-for-Machine-Learning-130040.aspx

AI for Business
http://images.learn.workfusion.com/Web/WorkFusion/%7B4ec36d2d-2fdf-4d55-a687-4476ea4f915b%7D_WSWF_LB5D_Raconteur_-_AI_For_Business_052118.pdf

AI Companies

For AI companies, see below in white papers or http://tsunami.ai/white-papers - and look for the list of top 100 AI companies. And of course,

google for "top AI companies _____" (whatever year it is) and "top AI startups _____" (ex: 2019, 2020, etc.)
Also: https://www.cbinsights.com/research/artificial-intelligence-top-startups/

Emerging/Related Technology

Driverless Cars
Why you have (probably) already bought your last car
https://www.bbc.com/news/business-45786690

Drones
drones + planes = bad
https://m.youtube.com/watch?v=QH0V7kp-xg0

Inspiration: Opportunities (and Jobs) in AI

AI and Science

A new approach to detecting cancer earlier from blood tests
https://www.sciencedaily.com/releases/2018/11/181114132000.htm
Cancer scientists have combined 'liquid biopsy,' epigenetic alterations and machine learning to develop a blood test to detect and classify cancer at its earliest stages.
Note: Science Daily is an awesome site. I recommend bookmarking it!

A.I. Is Helping Scientists Predict When and Where the Next Big Earthquake Will Be
https://www.nytimes.com/2018/10/26/technology/earthquake-predictions-artificial-intelligence.html

A nice article showing how AI-assisted robotics could help with prosthetic limbs https://www.nytimes.com/interactive/2018/07/30/technology/robot-hands.html?

This is VR, but it is still cool. I'm sure there will be a bit of AI in their somewhere.
https://www.technologyreview.com/s/612247/nasa-is-using-hololens-ar-headsets-to-build-its-new-spacecraft-faster/

Jobs/Careers in AI/Data Science/Machine Learning

Jobs in Data Science: data analysts, data scientists, data engineers
https://www.datacamp.com/community/blog/data-engineering
> Important discussion to help you understand the kinds of jobs that exist in AI. Keep in mind that this will change over time. At the present time, jobs in AI are dominated by roles requiring a "theoretical" understanding of AI: all the math, coding and other foundations; but over time as data science and AI flow from academic programs into applied use in business, there will be more "applied" roles. The article above talks about the industry using the language of data science, but other related job titles include Machine Learning Engineer. To help understand the kind of roles available, I invite you to go to indeed.com and jobs on Linkedin, and search for various keywords, including the titles above. You might also want to look at salaries in indeed as well as on salary.com

Future-proof your IT career with these critical skills
https://www.cio.com/article/3268945/it-skills-training/future-proof-your-it-career-with-these-critical-skills.html#tk.drr_mlt
In the era of digital transformation, IT pros must adjust to a rapidly shifting technology and business landscape. Here's a long-term look at where to aim your career in the years ahead.

Demand for AI talent exploding: Here are the 10 most in-demand jobs
https://www.techrepublic.com/article/demand-for-ai-talent-exploding-here-are-the-10-most-in-demand-jobs/
Employer demand for AI-related roles has more than doubled over the past three years, according to Indeed.

At the present time, and probably for the near to mid-term, there is a severe shortage of AI, deep learning and neural network talent. To give you some idea of the consequences:

How much should I charge per hour for a deep learning consulting job?
https://www.quora.com/How-much-should-I-charge-per-hour-for-a-deep-learning-consulting-job

Careers in Data Science

Understanding Data Science and Why It's So Important
https://blog.alexa.com/know-data-science-important/https://blog.alexa.com/know-data-science-important/
It's been said that Data Scientist is the"sexiest job title of the 21st century." Why is it such a demanded position these days? The short answer is that over the last decade there's been a massive explosion in both the data generated and retained by companies, as well as you and me. Sometimes we call this "big data," and like a pile of lumber we'd like to build something with it. Data scientists are the people who make sense out of all this data and figure out just what can be done with it.

My Journey Into Data Science
https://towardsdatascience.com/my-journey-into-data-science-39e9bbbbf452

Day in the Life: Data Scientist
https://www.youtube.com/watch?v=_Wk9T_G-u4o
In this episode of our "Day in the Life" series, Chevron Data Scientist Alena Crivello describes her use of analytics to find solutions to complex problems.

Career Transition Towards Data Analytics & Science. Here's my Story
https://www.datasciencecentral.com/profiles/blogs/career-transition-towards-data-analytics-amp-science-here-s-my

The Role of Statistics in Data Science

https://community.amstat.org/blogs/ronald-wasserstein/2015/10/01/the-role-of-statistics-in-data-science-an-asa-statement

". . . statistics is foundational to data science—along with database management and distributed and parallel systems—and its use in this emerging field empowers researchers to extract knowledge and obtain better results from big Data and other analytics projects. The statement also encourages maximum and multifaceted collaboration between statisticians and data scientists to maximize the full potential of data science."

AI For Social Good

Really good article on using AI for good; may be inspiring to workers, students, educators and provide some ideas for areas to pursue, or futures to create.

https://utterbuzz.com/2018/10/ai-for-social-good/

AI Optimism/Job Creation

There are definitely people who believe that AI will result in net job creation, and that AI is pretty much for the better. To me the book Master Algorithm is a key example - that book inspired me when I was alarmed, and helped me cross over into *wanting* to learn AI.

https://www.technologyreview.com/s/611805/the-four-ways-that-ex-internet-idealists-explain-where-it-all-went-wrong/

Google DeepMind founder Demis Hassabis: Three truths about AI
https://www.techrepublic.com/article/google-deepmind-founder-demis-hassabis-three-truths-about-ai/
One of the creators of the AI research company famed for building the pioneering AlphaGo AI spells out the technology's impact and future development.

The New Form of Intelligence You'll Need

https://www.usnews.com/news/best-countries/articles/2018-06-22/human-iq-and-artificial-intelligence-can-work-together-business-professor-says
Artificial intelligence and human IQ might be what schools and employers will be looking for in the future.

From rust belt to robot belt: Turning AI into jobs in the US heartland
https://www.technologyreview.com/s/611412/ai-could-wreak-economic-havoc-we-need-more-of-it/
Artificial intelligence is offering an amazing opportunity to increase prosperity, but whether or not we will seize it is our choice.

https://www.wsj.com/articles/seven-jobs-robots-will-createor-expand-1525054021

An optimist view of net job growth for AI, and expected in-demand jobs
http://techgenix.com/in-demand-it-positions/amp/

Optimist Viewpoint on WEF Study

Most of the studies I've seen indicate there will be significant job loss from AI - but in some cases the same study will say different things to different people. I also believe it's important to consider opposing viewpoints.

Here's an example of an optimist blurb from a World Economic Forum study:

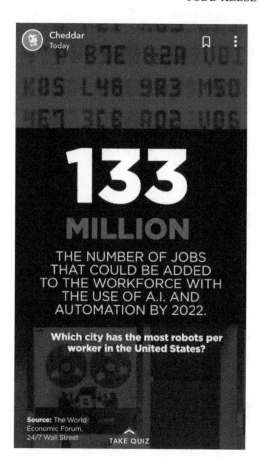

https://247wallst.com/economy/2018/09/17/rise-of-machines-and-ai-could-add-133-million-jobs/

Job Creation
https://www.forbes.com/sites/amitchowdhry/2018/09/18/artificial-intelligence-to-create-58-million-new-jobs-by-2022-says-report/#392b9a8a4d4b

Learn AI

60 Second Suggestion: download datacamp, codeacademy, mimo, and check out the free Google courses.

My general suggestion is to explore and try. Read through some of the options below, and try some.

I think it's worth watching videos and reading about machine learning (including applications of AI, mentioned in the book), deep learning, even if you aren't "ready". As mentioned in the review of Master Algorithm - that got me inspired to want to learn how to actually do it. When you start wanting to get into it directly, there are some pre-requisites, and if you reach that milestone, I still recommend making a sandwich out of it - continuing to learn about the high level (deep learning, machine learning), and learning the pre-requisites in parallel: coding, linear algebra, basic probability, statistics). Ideally, when learning the pre-requisites, trying to find material that is focused on the *context* of machine learning - that is, not just the "entirety" of linear algebra for example (because you might feel overwhelmed); but when possible, looking for material that helps you learn math "for" machine learning, to make it more focused. I think it is the same for coding: even though general introductions are good, when possible try to find material on "coding for machine learning" or "python for data science" or "python for deep learning", and if you get in over your head, file it away, learn, and come back for more.

- Apps: For me, a starting point has just been to download some of the apps, like datacamp, codeacademy, mimo - and just spend a few minutes exploring after dinner.
- Games: Because I have to brush up on my linear algebra, I found the very popular app Dragonbox. I'm trying to find more games that teach the relevant topics in AI (please let me know if you know of any - http://tsunami.ai/contact)
- Videos: I've also found videos a nice way to learn - the 3Blue1Brown videos on linear algebra and the series on deep learning are very popular, and helpful.
- Buddies: When possible, find others to go through the journey with you.
- Meetups: Meetups are a great way to learn and to find inspiration and encouragement (as well as to ask questions and even find jobs)
- Classes: when possible, I think in-person classes are best. If your school or community college or college doesn't have any - ask them to! I think in-person classes are the best way to learn because of the structure, the human dimension, the ability to ask questions, and the direct mentorship.

- Online classes: I think online classes are a great way to learn, to supplement in-person classes, or when they aren't feasible. In addition to teaching in-person classes, I teach (and take) online classes.
- Post/Blog/Share: when possible, I recommend sharing how things are going for you on social media. Don't worry about being an expert. You may be surprised by the encouragement you'll find when you share, on personal networks and messaging apps like Facebook, Twitter, Instagram, Pinterest, whatever - or more professional networks. I'm guessing you'll also find other people who want to learn.

Google AI Education (free)

Learn from ML experts at Google
https://ai.google/education/
Whether you're just learning to code or you're a seasoned machine learning practitioner, you'll find information and exercises to help you develop your skills and advance your projects.

Amazon (free, and paid)

Amazon's own 'Machine Learning University' now available to all developers
https://aws.amazon.com/blogs/machine-learning/amazons-own-machine-learning-university-now-available-to-all-developers/
https://aws.amazon.com/training/learning-paths/machine-learning/
(includes paths for business decision makers)
Plus certification: aws.training/machinelearning

Kaggle
Kaggle.com is a good all around resource. There are learning tutorials, and there are also live projects, competitions, and a sense of community. One prominent data scientists told me that he highly recommended kaggle.
http://kaggle.com

AI for Everyone - AI Expert Andrew Ng - (paid)
https://venturebeat.com/2018/11/13/andrew-ng-launches-ai-for-everyone-a-new-coursera-program-aimed-at-business-professionals/
Andrew Ng launches 'AI for Everyone,' a new Coursera program aimed at business professionals
> Coursera has an audit option for many but not all of their courses

General Topics

Machine Learning

Machine Learning Basics
https://www.datacamp.com/community/news/machine-learning-basics-a9h0fv91cqs

Trading platform example (using machine learning to automate trading)
https://www.datacamp.com/community/news/development-of-cloud-based-automated-trading-system-with-machine-learn-7ma1qjwer9y

Introductions to Deep Learning, Neural Networks

But what *is* a Neural Network? | Deep learning, chapter 1
https://www.youtube.com/watch?v=aircAruvnKk&t=468s
> in the Show More/Description area there is more information and a link to a free book he recommends reading.
> Also in the series of videos he recommends a number of resources

Note: this same author has a really good series on linear algebra, which is one of the pre-requisites for the current generation of machine learning.

Some Beginner Intros and Series:

Beginner Intro to Neural Networks 1: Data and Graphing

https://www.youtube.com/watch?v=ZzWaow1Rvho&list=PLxt59R
_fWVzT9bDxA76AHm3ig0Gg9S3So

A friendly introduction to Recurrent Neural Networks
https://www.youtube.com/watch?v=UNmqTiOnRfg

Math for Machine Learning
As assistive platforms arise, there may be less need for a better
understanding of math, but it is required for the current generation of
machine learning and AI. The general types of math related to deep learning
and machine learning are basic probability and statistics, linear algebra.

Math in Data Science
https://www.dataquest.io/blog/math-in-data-science/

Learn Math for machine learning.
https://www.kaggle.com/getting-started/59541
--
blogs
https://towardsdatascience.com/the-mathematics-of-machine-
learning-894f046c568
https://blog.ycombinator.com/learning-math-for-machine-learning/
https://medium.com/technomancy/the-math-required-for-machine-
learning-af0d90db3903
--
videos
https://www.youtube.com/watch?v=8onB7rPG4Pk&vl=en
--
PDF
https://courses.washington.edu/css490/2012.Winter/lecture_slides/
02_math_essentials.pdf

--
intermediate
https://www.edx.org/course/essential-math-for-machine-learning-
python-edition

--

live online course ($1,250 USD)
https://www.thisismetis.com/courses/beginner-python-and-math-for-data-science#overview

Codeacademy

https://www.codecademy.com/catalog/subject/all

Learning coding is closely tied to AI, data science and machine learning. DataCamp, Coursera and Udacity all have intro courses for programming - and Codeacademy is a primary resource that many use, for free and paid coding courses.

Like other providers, there are nice apps you can download, as well as online options.

Below are some of the options

COURSES

Codecademy courses teach you a technical skill through interactive lessons. Practice projects and quizzes are available for our Pro members.

Course

Welcome To Codecademy

First time on our site? Start here to learn how to use our platform

Course

Learn How to Code

Learn key programming concepts and write your first lines of code!

Course

Introduction to HTML

In just 4 hours, learn the basics of HTML5 and start building & ed...

PRO_ Exclusive Course

Learn Python 3

Learn the latest and greatest version of the most popular programmin...

Course

Learn Python 2

Learn the basics of the world's fastest growing and most popular

Course

Introduction To JavaScript

Learn the JavaScript fundamentals you'll need for front-end or back-...

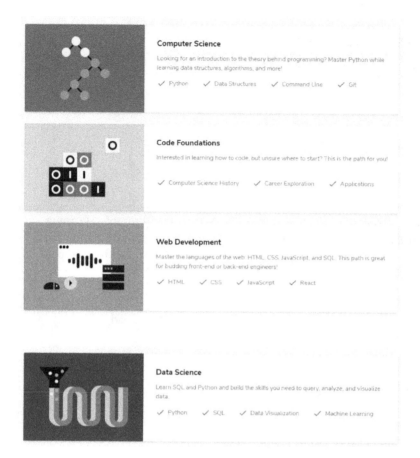

As you grow in your learning, Codeacademy (and Coursera/Udacity) have more advanced and intensive courses. If you are working somewhere, you might be able to get some assistance from your employer. Want some help proposing that? http://tsunami.ai/contact

INTENSIVE PROGRAMS   INTENSIVE

Each Codecademy program is designed to upgrade your skills through a rigorous curriculum with personalized support. Level up today!

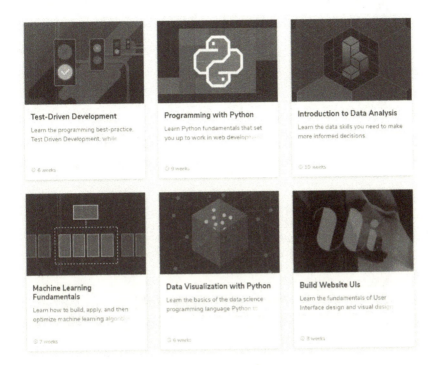

DataCamp App/Courses

I like Datacamp. Datacamp has a really good intro free app, and good free online courses.

An email below from Nov 2018, some of the promoted courses are intermediate level but they also have intros.

Analyzing Social Media sounds fun, and maybe inspiring to students. Basing data science education on Google Sheets is nice since it is free. I think that starting at the spreadsheet level for data science makes a lot of sense, because it is an easier platform, and may already be familiar to some people. (Google Sheets is a free online alternative to Microsoft Excel - you can access it free and many other tools by starting a google account/gmail account.)

We're launching eight new courses, including two new spreadsheet courses. Intermediate Spreadsheets for Data Science will expand your Google Sheets vocabulary. You'll dive deep into data types, practice manipulating numeric and logical data, and much more. We are also launching Pivot Tables with Spreadsheets. In this course, you'll explore the world of Pivot Tables within Google Sheets, and learn how to quickly organize thousands of data points with just a few clicks of the mouse.

Finally, check out five courses that are top rated by other DataCamp users.

New Courses:
- *Intermediate Spreadsheets for Data Science*
- *Pivot Tables with Spreadsheets*
- *Visualizing Geospatial Data in Python*
- *Dealing with Missing Data in R*
- *Designing and Analyzing Clinical Trials in R*
- *Financial Analytics in R*
- *Foundation of Functional Programming with purrr (in R)*
- *Network Science: A Tidy Approach (in R)*

5 Courses Recommended by Other DataCamp Users
- *Multiple and Logistic Regression (in R)*
- *Introduction to Time Series Analysis in Python*
- *Machine Learning Toolbox (in R)*
- *Text Mining: Bag of Words (in R)*
- *Analyzing Social Media Data in Python*

See: https://www.datacamp.com/courses

Coursera - free or paid (also look up Udacity)

Coursera has an audit option for many but not all of their courses. Both Coursera and Udacity have a variety of courses, certificates and even degrees available in relation to AI and machine learning. (ex: sponsored by AT&T and given through Georgia Tech and Udacity, there is a Master's Degree in Computer Science with a Specialization in Machine Learning, which is significantly less expensive than other Master's Degrees.)

Re: auditing (i.e. free)

https://learner.coursera.help/hc/en-us/articles/209818613-Enrollment-options

https://www.coursera.org/specializations/mathematics-machine-learning

https://www.coursera.org/learn/linear-algebra-machine-learning

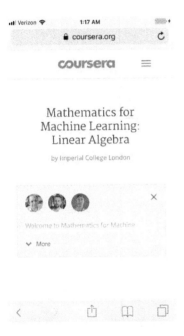

Mimo

Mimo is an app for learning coding. I'm impressed.

| Mimo has a nice format | And good feedback |

| It is interactive and uses familiar items to build coding concepts. | Legos are an excellent metaphor. It is said that programmers sometimes actually find them |

	helpful in thinking about modularity

Data Science

Data scientists weigh in: 5 data science tools to consider (August 2018)
The surge of data captured by today's organizations requires data science tools to fully understand the information. We asked data scientists what tools they're using.
https://searchbusinessanalytics.techtarget.com/feature/Data-scientists-weigh-in-5-data-science-tools-to-consider

LinkedIN (free trial, subscription)
https://www.linkedin.com/learning/python-for-data-science-essential-training
> and many other courses

AI Realism: Understand AI's Impact on Jobs

The June 2018 Financial Times article on Citi seems to me like one of the most important articles in 2018 in regards to job impact - it made one of the biggest impressions on me, serving as evidence that AI-driven automation is *already* having a *significant* impact on jobs.

Finance

June 2018 report that Citi expects to shed 20,000 jobs
Citi issues stark warning on automation of bank jobs | Financial Times
https://www.ft.com/content/579c977c-6d73-11e8-92d3-6c13e5c92914
Jun 11, 2018 - Citigroup's investment bank has suggested that it will shed up to half of its 20,000 technology and operations staff in the next five years

Personal

How to Survive AI
http://cmr.berkeley.edu/blog/2018/10/how-to-survive-ai/

F.I.R.E.: Financial Independence, Retire Early

There is a movement among some people who can do it, to try and be frugal, earn as much as possible and seek to retire early.
https://www.nytimes.com/2018/09/01/style/fire-financial-independence-retire-early.html

This is the paragraph that caught my eye. So these are well-paid tech sector people we're talking about.

> *Though they had good educations and well-paying jobs in the booming tech sector, Ms. Shen and Mr. Leung faced the looming threats of outsourcing and artificial intelligence, and had no hope of a retirement pension, or even that their employers would exist in five years.*

Retail

Good video
https://www.wsj.com/video/series/a-brief-history-of/a-brief-history-of-retail/F1AE7DC6-BB25-499C-9A2A-D120C18C3798

https://www.cbinsights.com/research/cashierless-retail-technologies-companies-trends/

Healthcare

Google's AI is better at spotting advanced breast cancer than pathologists

https://www.technologyreview.com/the-download/612292/googles-ai-is-better-at-spotting-advanced-breast-cancer-than-pathologists/
The firm's deep-learning tool was able to correctly distinguish metastatic cancer 99% of the time, a greater accuracy rate than human pathologists.

AI is making significant inroads into health. On the good side, there are many medical discoveries waiting to happen, and already happening, because of the significant power AI has to process medical data, scientific data, and help build solutions. It is one reason there was a big controversy over Google seeking to obtain and develop a massive database of cancer related information - then the hospital in question backed out and tried to develop it themselves.

Sloan Kettering's Cozy Deal With Start-Up Ignites a New Uproar
https://www.nytimes.com/2018/09/20/health/memorial-sloan-kettering-cancer-paige-ai.html

I'm pretty confident medical research is one of the biggest opportunities for AI - could it help cure cancer? Or _____?

And on the other hand, the power of AI will probably reduce the need for medical staff. AI has already proven to be more effective than doctors at diagnosis, because it can compare symptoms to a massive medical database. It is true there will likely always be a need for a human element, and AI Expert Kai Fu Lee recognizes the massive job loss will bring in all fields, and has an interesting perspective - he believes in encourage the growth and creation of jobs involving empathy - including health caregiving. So there is some opportunity.

It will be an ongoing debate.

https://www.nytimes.com/interactive/2018/05/16/magazine/health-issue-what-we-lose-with-data-driven-medicine.html

Automation/Manufacturing

Automation is not always a clear-cut issue. Labor shortage can lead to automation. (But that's still jobs that could have been done by humans) https://www.wsj.com/articles/companies-ramp-up-worker-retraining-efforts-1535889600?mod=mhp

The realities of what some people are facing:

Why robots helped Donald Trump win
Toledo has more robots per worker than any other US city. They're producing a healthy economy—and lots of anxiety.
https://www.technologyreview.com/s/611422/why-robots-helped-donald-trump-win/

—

Some Toledo-area leaders might realize that a technological meteor is headed their way. But what are they supposed to do about something so unpredictable in its details? So they stress "lifelong learning." From the junior high kids in the robotics camp to the factory-floor employee, they all have to turn their lives into one long hustle to keep their heads above the incoming tide and whatever it might wash in.

—

"We used to laugh at the robots," Rickey's buddy said. "When they first came in, they were so slow. We would sorta hurry and outproduce them. But one of the lines was about 18 people, and now they can run it with, like, five."

—

Rickey looked at me and said he tells his own children that if they wind up working in the plant, "then I failed as a father."

New autonomous farm wants to produce food without human workers
https://www.technologyreview.com/s/612230/new-autonomous-farm-wants-to-produce-food-without-human-workers/

Down on a new robot farm, machines tend rows of leafy greens under the watch of software called "The Brain."

Digital Marketing

The original reason why I wrote Surfing the Tsunami is because of teaching digital marketing and starting to wonder throughout 2017 if, or when, digital marketing jobs might be replaced with AI. That led to everything else, including me taking my own medicine, and learning more about data science, AI, linear algebra, Python, machine learning, etc. Frederick Vallaeys is the CEO of Optmyzr.com, whose articles helped inform the beginning of my journey; and the articles continued.

Are the Days of Human-Managed PPC Numbered?
https://www.searchenginejournal.com/automation-human-managed-ppc/252255/

Digital Marketing: The Vallaeys Scale (my term)

Frederick's comments are about digital marketing specifically, but similar evolution and automation will be affecting every other field.

Todd: So I want to call your automation scale the Vallaeys Scale, kind of like the Richter Scale. Care to give me an estimate of the number we were are at based on dates?

Jan 2017
https://searchengineland.com/artificial-intelligence-drives-ppc-automation-267561
3.0?

May 2018
https://www.searchenginejournal.com/automation-human-managed-ppc/252255
3.5?

August 18
3.6?

AutoML feels to me like the biggest wildcard.

Fred: Nice, I hope people can spell that :-)

I think around 2017 we were at a level 2 because advertisers had to choose from a slew of automation components for each campaign. It did not appear that the automations talked to each other though they did react to what was happening as a result of other automations.

Now (Aug 18) we're at a level 3 where 'smart campaigns' from Google handle lots of aspects in an interconnected way. Smart shopping campaigns may indeed be at a 3.5 because thanks to existing structured data, Google basically knows what is being sold and generates even the ads so there's almost nothing that a human has to do (though there is still lots they can do to improve results)

I don't know I'd put May 18 in a separate bucket. I think a lot of the automations from Google then were still level-2 point solutions.

AutoML is scary interesting though. Could be a game changer!

Talk soon!
Fred Vallaeys
Cofounding CEO

Automation of Writing

Computer Stories: A.I. Is Beginning to Assist Novelists
https://www.nytimes.com/2018/10/18/technology/ai-is-beginning-to-assist-

novelists.html?action=click&module=Discovery&pgtype=Homepag
e

More on AI's Impact on Jobs

Watch Out Workers, Algorithms Are Coming to Replace You — Maybe
https://www.nytimes.com/2018/10/18/business/q-and-a-yuval-harari.html

Adapt or die: How to cope when the bots take your job
http://www.bbc.com/news/business-43259906

As the company builds up the number of tasks it can automate, it's slowly creating a computerized employee.
https://www.technologyreview.com/the-download/611922/ai-powered-software-robots-are-getting-into-the-sales-business/

https://www.wsj.com/articles/whats-on-your-mind-bosses-are-using-artificial-intelligence-to-find-out-1522251302

AI Realism: Understand RPA/Bots

I think robotic process automation is both assisting and destroying many jobs; my tentative view is that RPA is inevitable and inexorable. Attempts to regulate it would probably fail, because other countries would not regulate it and have an economic advantage, and protections would probably eventually be limited or reduced, either by pressure, or companies moving outside the sphere of regulation, or the stagnation of an economy that tried to resist AI. I don't claim to have the answers, nor am I hostile to RPA. I think I might feel queasy working in a consultancy that was helping to implement it, if a significant number of jobs were to be lost - yet I think it is inevitable, and I'm considering inviting my students to get certified in WorkFusion, for example. Workfusion is mentioned in the alarmist book Rise of The Robots, where it talks about how the robotic process automation engines can be trained by Ivy League grads in sophisticated tasks, to the point where their input is no longer needed. Yet it is also true that automation technology can be assistive - but it still seems to exert considerable force in a likely shrinking of the number of people required to do a particular job, even if a company expands.

So I'd recommend looking at it closely. Robotic Process Automation for me would fit into the Adopt stage of Adapt > Adopt > Adept, ideally where students, workers might have a chance to become the ones who would be managing a platform rather than being replaced by it.

The Big RPA Bubble
https://www.forbes.com/sites/cognitiveworld/2018/12/02/the-big-rpa-bubble/
> This is a really interesting article - it's aimed at the people implementing robotic process automation, and it seems to be a foregone conclusion that jobs will be replaced. You can infer a lot simply by reading the article.
"What's the right way to implement RPA? Instead of trying to build a program around staff reduction and thinking about how to achieve 100 percent automation to replace a handful of FTEs, focus on some level of basic task automation for every staff member . . . "

"Robotic Process Automation (RPA). It's a hot topic among the C-Suite. Where to implement. How to implement. How many headcounts can be saved through robotic implementations?"

Machine Learning and RPA (Video)
> from a promo email. Video link here: https://tinyurl.com/rpa2-vid or below.

Super smart analysts are the closest things we have to crystal balls in the business world, and Forrester's Craig Le Clair is one of the brightest crystal balls in Intelligent Automation.

In this free, on-demand webinar, RPA 2.0: the new operation model for scaling and the critical role of analytics, Craig explains:

- *How the next generation of RPA leverages machine learning (ML) to scale automation*

- *How the future business landscape will be impacted by ML-powered automation*
- *Why it's critical for enterprises to start their transformation initiatives now*

RPA Value Proposition from a promotional email

Our CEO, Alex Lyashok, just announced the launch of Lumen, WorkFusion's Intelligent Automation 2018 release, which delivers major upgrades to our flagship AI-driven RPA product, Smart Process Automation (SPA), and starter product RPA Express.

The Lumen release aims to make AI simple and powerful for everyone through four core themes:
- ***Simpler RPA:*** *One-click install and faster bot performance.*
- ***Everyday AI:*** *Out-of-the-box machine learning for business people.*
- ***Enterprise-grade:*** *Centralized and secure credential management for IT compliance.*
- ***Analytics:*** *Deeper insights that predict cost, quality, and productivity.*

I'd suggest playing with WorkFusion, including RPA Express, in order to understand it better, including perhaps going through the exercise of manually doing a particular task, timing yourself, and then using RPA express to automate the task.

Automation is definitely a thing. There's even an Automation Anywhere bot Hackathon. And some pitfalls and things to keep in mind when developing and deploying them.
https://blogs.wsj.com/cio/2018/05/29/bots-can-break-leaving-corporate-tasks-undone/

Here is another Workfusion marketing excerpt. This is the kind of material enterprise management is reviewing in consideration of Robotic Process Automation.

--

Hi Todd, Everest Group consistently delivers excellent research on enterprise technology to help businesses adapt and transform. Their latest report, Creating Business Value Through Next-Generation Digital

Workforce, is no exception, and we've licensed it so that you can freely download it.

You'll learn the following:
The problems with the current workforce model
The different types of bots that comprise a digital workforce
Why the combination of RPA and cognitive automation is superior to either on its own
--
http://images.learn.workfusion.com/Web/WorkFusion/%7Bb557a7
f0-71a5-4336-a31e-
5cdcc2bbd2b3%7D_2017_10_everest_group_next-
gen_digital_workforce.pdf

Why AI Is Unpredictable: Quantum AI

Quantum AI is not the only reason advances in AI are unpredictable, but long-term, it's a major issue. AI and machine learning could become more sophisticated as a result of quantum computing. That is partly why my view is that automation powered by AI (and/or quantum computing) *could replace jobs much more quickly than anyone predicts*. Experts in AI, even optimists, usually are careful to qualify their predictions, exactly because of wildcards like quantum computing.

So get in touch with your inner science, and keep an eye on quantum!

Case in point - an area to watch - machine learning and quantum computing:

Machine learning, meet quantum computing
https://www.technologyreview.com/s/612435/machine-learning-
meet-quantum-computing/
A quantum version of the building block behind neural networks could be exponentially more powerful.

Why Most of Us Fail to Grasp Coming Exponential Gains in AI

https://singularityhub.com/2018/07/15/why-most-of-us-fail-to-grasp-coming-exponential-gains-in-ai
> A really good article that shows the unpredictability of the advances (which is why I think it is important to take AI so seriously.

Quantum AI

One very large wildcard in artificial intelligence which could radically change every assumption that has been made about "pacing" in the sophistication of AI, job replacement, etc., is quantum computing. There are some scientists who don't believe that quantum computing will ever actually take off - but companies and governments are watching it very, very closely.

And of course - it could be quite wonderful for science too - in terms of helping solve questions and making advances that may be too complex to fully figure out at present. Cancer, Space Exploration, Climate Change, etc.

Ex: Climate Change and AI - 2.17.19
https://www.oxfordstudent.com/2019/02/17/climate-change-the-case-for-artificial-intelligence/

Inspiration: If you like fiction, try reading the Quantum Spy:
https://www.amazon.com/Quantum-Spy-Thriller-David-Ignatius/dp/0393254151)

By pacing, I mean that if/when quantum computing becomes more practical (billions are being poured into exactly this pursuit), the pace of increasing sophistication in AI and robotics may increase beyond anyone's expectations. The existence of quantum computing is one of the reasons I think any prediction of something that "AI can never do" is *very* uncertain.

So my recommendation is try to keep an eye on quantum computing. Maybe by regularly looking at a site like Quanta.com. Or simply by keeping your eyes on sources of information like MIT Technology Review.

The world's first quantum software superstore—or so it hopes—is here
https://www.technologyreview.com/s/611139/the-worlds-first-quantum-software-superstore-or-so-it-hopes-is-here/
Zapata Computing plans to build the algorithms for companies that want to experiment with quantum computers.

The Argument Against Quantum Computers
https://www.quantamagazine.org/gil-kalais-argument-against-quantum-computers-20180207/
The mathematician Gil Kalai believes that quantum computers can't possibly work, even in principle.

With all the changes that have already happened with AI, and the disruption that is expected to continue happening, it's also important to note that there is a viewpoint that quantum computing in and of itself will be more disruptive than AI.

Quantum Computing, not AI, will Define Our Future
https://techcrunch.com/2018/11/17/quantum-computing-not-ai-will-define-our-future/

Studies

Studies that got my attention that I think are worth considering.

(World Economic Forum)
Machines will do more work than humans by 2025, says the WEF - Sept 2018
In less than a decade, most workplace tasks will be done by machines rather than humans, according to the World Economic Forum's latest AI job forecast.
https://www.technologyreview.com/the-download/612121/machines-will-do-more-work-than-humans-by-2025-says-the-wef/

Notes from the AI frontier: Modeling the impact of AI on the world economy - Sept 2018

Artificial intelligence has large potential to contribute to global economic activity. But widening gaps among countries, companies, and workers will need to be managed to maximize the benefits. The role of artificial intelligence (AI) tools and techniques in business and the global economy is a hot topic. This is not surprising given that AI might usher in radical—arguably unprecedented—changes in the way people live and work. The AI revolution is not in its infancy, but most of its economic impact is yet to come. https://www.mckinsey.com/featured-insights/artificial-intelligence/notes-from-the-frontier-modeling-the-impact-of-ai-on-the-world-economy

Education - Implications of AI

Note: I am making Surfing the Tsunami available free to any educator, staff member and all of their students - http://tsunami.ai/edu

I believe there is an important need for schools and colleges to explore how AI and data science can help prepare students for jobs in the future. I believe it is an interdisciplinary question, and leading schools are blazing a path. The president of MIT called on the country and education to help students in all disciplines to become AI bilingual - to develop fluency in data and artificial intelligence. It's not just a question for a computer science department. For example, a business department can bring business applications of AI and underlying analytics to the table. (Ex: digital marketing automation.)

If you are an educator, staff member, student or concerned citizen, some of these articles may be helpful in starting discussion around these issues.

Impact of AI on Higher Education
http://tsunami.ai/white-papers
> This is a pretty easy to read visual presentation I gave at a 2018 academic conference, based on the themes in Surfing the Tsunami. It might be helpful as a class presentation or just to get acquainted with the topic.

Rafael Reif, President of MIT

Fact: MIT is seeking to help students in *every discipline* to increase their technical skills and to leverage AI

Implication: you don't have to be MIT to come to the same conclusion, and personally I think collaboration is necessary between schools, all their departments, companies and governments around the world to help students in any school to learn more, as well as anyone, of any age, who is not currently in school. That's the main reason I wrote this book.

The President of MIT's official release calling on education and government to support AI, as well as interdisciplinary AI education. http://news.mit.edu/2019/president-reif-oped-federal-opportunity-and-threat-ai-0211

A related opinion piece he wrote discussing AI bilinguality: https://www.ft.com/content/24f18c28-2a39-11e9-9222-7024d72222bc

A nice video clip from Switzerland (brrr!) with the same message: http://news.mit.edu/news-clip/clip-wsj-large-artificial-intelligence-will-be-part-college-curriculum-mit-president

Joseph Aoun, President of Northeastern University

With Changing Students and Times, Colleges Are Going Back to School
https://mobile.nytimes.com/2018/04/05/education/learning/colleges-adapt-changing-students.html

(Comment from Todd: The kind of information pointed to by the excerpt below leads me to believe that facing this issue is an urgent question; the bolded statement (my bold) seems to additional confirmation that this is a *now* issue, not a future issue.)

———

That keeps Joseph E. Aoun, president of Northeastern University in Boston, up at night. While other presidents in local college towns worry about competing for endowments and enrollment, Mr. Aoun sees another threat: robots.

More than the latest polls, he is driven by a 2013 Oxford University Study that predicted that nearly half of the jobs in the United States are at risk of being taken over by computers within the next two decades. "We said if robots are going to replace human beings we need to help students to be robot-proof, and we built a strategic plan around that," Mr. Aoun said.

That thinking positioned Mr. Aoun on the fringe of higher education strategizing just a few years ago, **but he is now called on weekly to advise other institutions on how to help their students outsmart the workers of the future.**

--

When it comes to lifelong learning, are universities the providers of last resort?
https://www.linkedin.com/pulse/when-comes-lifelong-learning-universities-providers-last-joseph-aoun/
> A good article that talks about the implications of AI on the job market as well as the need for lifelong learning for those who either never had college or graduated from college.
He even used the word tsunami!

--

It is no longer debatable that artificial intelligence will transform our economy; the only question is the precise size of the tsunami. Numerous studies predict that up to 50 percent of today's jobs will disappear over the next two decades. In developing economies it could be up to 70 percent.

These same forces will create new jobs that we can't even dream of today. But those jobs alone will not be sufficient: Just one in 10 workers are currently employed in fields that are projected to grow. Additionally, more than one in three existing jobs will require entirely different skill sets in the future.

--

Five Rules of the College and Career Game
https://cew.georgetown.edu/cew-reports/5rules/
As postsecondary education and training has become the most well-traveled pathway to middle class earnings, students, their families, and educators need to learn five rules of the college and career game. And sometimes those rules are contradictory.
> Report, a PDF, and interactive tool. Information on salaries of different majors, etc.

UC Berkeley's Fastest-Growing Class Is Data Science 101
https://www.wsj.com/articles/at-berkeley-its-big-data-on-campus-1541066401

Government/Public Policy

Free for Government People: I am making Surfing the Tsunami available free to any legislator or government staff member, at any level, in any government in the world - and all their constituents:
http://tsunami.ai/edu

Open Statement to Government: I believe it is crucial for any and every government to learn more about AI. If you know of any legislator who might be open to reading a book like Surfing the Tsunami, and how to get in touch with them, please let me know. For U.S. legislators I may be able to provide print copies, if not PDF copies, and I'm trying to find someone who could help me offer the book (and input) to every member of the

Congress and the Senate. If you know of a relevant organization or are convinced of the importance of AI and you want to help, please let me know! http://tsunami.ai/contact

What to Review: in addition to this section, government staff and legislators will probably want to review the sections in the book about thought leaders, education, etc.

The President of MIT's official release calling on education and government to support AI, as well as interdisciplinary AI education. http://news.mit.edu/2019/president-reif-oped-federal-opportunity-and-threat-ai-0211

A related opinion piece he wrote discussing AI bilinguality: https://www.ft.com/content/24f18c28-2a39-11e9-9222-7024d72222bc

A nice video clip from Switzerland (brrr!) with the same message: http://news.mit.edu/news-clip/clip-wsj-large-artificial-intelligence-will-be-part-college-curriculum-mit-president

National/International

Kai Fu Lee's New Book: AI Superpowers

I think Kai Fu Lee's book is worth reading, to learn more about how AI works, the related issues, and opportunities for the future for individuals and countries. In the presentation I attended in Chicago in September of 2019, Kai explained that the publisher pushed for the stark national imagery on the cover. But as a person Kai Fu Lee is mild-mannered, and his perspective is very valuable. The book does touch on international themes - but the conclusions are not really "us vs them" - one of the most interesting conclusions is the interesting idea that governments can and should encourage the development of jobs requiring compassion and empathy.

(See the CBS 60 Minutes video and articles mentioned in the Leaders section.)

https://www.amazon.com/AI-Superpowers-China-Silicon-Valley/dp/0358105587

Note: it's the #1 release in Government Management, and #1 in other categories.

State Government

Millions of Californians' jobs could be affected by automation — a scenario the next governor has to address
https://www.latimes.com/projects/la-pol-ca-next-california-work/

U.S. Government

https://www.technologyreview.com/s/611118/the-white-house-says-a-new-ai-taskforce-will-keep-america-first-and-protect-its-workers/

Universal Basic Income

(ex: when job losses increase, could UBL be a solution)

https://www.technologyreview.com/the-download/611797/ontario-is-axing-its-test-of-universal-basic-income/

https://www.cnbc.com/amp/2018/02/20/richard-branson-a-i-will-make-universal-basic-income-necessary.html

Teaching AI

AI for Business (multiple sections including one on teaching AI)
http://images.learn.workfusion.com/Web/WorkFusion/%7B4ec36d2d-2fdf-4d55-a687-4476ea4f915b%7D_WSWF_LB5D_Raconteur_-_AI_For_Business_052118.pdf

High School - Advance Placement Computer Science (which is aimed at an *interdisciplinary* audience)
https://www.nytimes.com/2019/02/12/opinion/college-board-sat-ap.html
"A few years ago, the leaders of the College Board, the folks who administer the SAT college entrance exam, asked themselves a radical question: Of all the skills and knowledge that we test young people for that we know are correlated with success in college and in life, which is the most important? Their answer: the ability to master "two codes" — computer science and the U.S. Constitution."
> Note: they are talking about **all** high school students.

Teaching AI - Practical vs Theoretical

Q: What would be the difference between using a pre-created library or set of functions, and needing to use more in depth math? Are you saying that for many high level, validated use cases, pre-created methods are sufficient, where only high level math is needed? Would it be fair to say that a deeper understanding of math is needed in order to customize for a particular context, or is the deeper understanding of math only needed for theoretical work where there is the need to develop new applied use cases?

A: In the textbook for my course, each ML algorithm is almost a line of code. The users only need to know what it does. Deeper understanding of math is of course helpful to understand the algorithms, but might not be needed. Understanding the math can enable more theoretical work.
Ex: http://www.jmlr.org/papers/v19/ and
https://arxiv.org/list/stat.ML/recent

Coding
A small team of student AI coders beats Google's machine-learning code
https://www.technologyreview.com/s/611858/small-team-of-ai-coders-beats-googles-code/
The success shows that advances in artificial intelligence aren't the sole domain of elite programmers.

Fun

I'm on a quest to find games that can help people learn math, coding, and even neural networks. The pickings are slim but the possibilities are huge. Please use tsunami.ai/contact if you know of anything, or would be interested in helping to either test or develop something.

https://github.com/ypwhs/NNPlayground

Whitepapers/Presentations/PDFs

This section has some of the PDFs that are available at
http://tsunami.ai/white-papers

Impact of AI on Higher Education

> This is a pretty easy to read simple presentation I gave at a 2018 academic conference, based on the themes in Surfing the Tsunami. It might be helpful as a class presentation or just to get acquainted with the topic.

Top 100 AI Companies 2018
> An interesting view of AI Startups and larger companies. Probably somewhat USA-centric.

Realizing the Benefits of Automated Machine Learning
> DataRobot is a company that is pursuing AutoML (not Google's AutoML, but their own variety) - in the hopes of making it easier to learn about and leverage AI at companies. DataRobot has a lot of good material and could help especially with people who don't necessarily have a computer science background.

Next Generation Digital Workforce
A 2018 report by Everest Group, targeting the enterprise, for WorkFusion, making the case for Robotic Process Automation.

Enterprise Artificial Intelligence (AI) Services 2018
> analysis by Accenture on enterprise AI

AWS (Amazon) Cloud Certification 2018
> I'm strongly in favor of certifications, I believe there should be multiple AI certifications (Please use the contact form if you're interested, if you know of one, or know anyone who'd like to help develop one)
> Amazon has a lot of educational material - at the present they have a "cloud" certification, which might be worth looking into. They also have AI training material, and a tool called Sagemaker. Amazon's products/training are one way to learn AI, like Google's similar tools/training material.

Market Guide for AI-Related Consulting and SI Services for Intelligent Automation
> enterprise level guide to give a sense of the kind of AI companies and consulting out there.

Data Integration and Machine Learning: A Natural Synergy

> This is a nuts and bolts guide that gets deep into the weeds on how data integration is important for implementation of AI at companies.

ABSTRACT: There is now more data to analyze than ever before. As data volume and variety have increased, so have the ties between machine learning and data integration become stronger. For machine learning to be effective, one must utilize data from the greatest possible variety of sources; and this is why data integration plays a key role. At the same time machine learning is driving automation in data integration, resulting in overall reduction of integration costs and improved accuracy. This tutorial focuses on three aspects of the synergistic relationship between data integration and machine learning: (1) we survey how state-of-the-art data integration solutions rely on machine learning-based approaches for accurate results and effective human-in-the-loop pipelines, (2) we review how end-to-end machine learning applications rely on data integration to identify accurate, clean, and relevant data for their analytics exercises, and (3) we discuss open research challenges and opportunities that span across data integration and machine learning.

(McKinsey)
MGI Notes from the AI frontier: Modeling the impact of AI on the world economy - Sept 2018
Artificial intelligence has large potential to contribute to global economic activity. But widening gaps among countries, companies, and workers will need to be managed to maximize the benefits. The role of artificial intelligence (AI) tools and techniques in business and the global economy is a hot topic. This is not surprising given that AI might usher in radical—arguably unprecedented—changes in the way people live and work. The AI revolution is not in its infancy, but most of its economic impact is yet to come.

International AI - China, Finland etc

If you know of or find resources in other languages and/or for other countries, please let me know: http://tsunami.ai/contact

Finland's grand AI experiment
Inside Finland's plan to train its population in artificial intelligence
https://www.politico.eu/article/finland-one-percent-ai-artificial-intelligence-courses-learning-training/

Inside the Chinese lab that plans to rewire the world with AI
Alibaba is investing huge sums in AI research and resources—and it is building tools to challenge Google and Amazon.

https://www.technologyreview.com/s/610219/inside-the-chinese-lab-that-plans-to-rewire-the-world-with-ai/

China's leaders are softening their stance on AI
A year after announcing an aggressive plan to dominate artificial intelligence, China's vice premier has called for international collaboration.
https://www.technologyreview.com/s/612141/chinas-leaders-are-calling-for-international-collaboration-on-ai/
> I happen to believe that science has no borders, and that international collaboration is crucially important, especially if you are in the majority of people who believe that climate change is a big problem. (Wouldn't it be nice to collaborate and help spare future generations from the consequences of climate change? And every other threat to health for that matter?)

Ex: Climate Change and AI - 2.17.19
https://www.oxfordstudent.com/2019/02/17/climate-change-the-case-for-artificial-intelligence/

Debate: AI Job Impact

https://www.wsj.com/articles/inside-the-new-industrial-revolution-1542040187?mod=mhp
—

(My Response)
To claim that " it is less about replacing workers" is misleading and inaccurate.

*The biggest gap in this analysis is the lack of mentioning how many jobs will be lost from automation of both routine tasks and sophisticated analysis. Large employers in their own words point to this, **such as the June 2018 report that Citi expects to shed 20,000 jobs.***

https://www.ft.com/content/579c977c-6d73-11e8-92d3-6c13e5c92914

There is no mention of the many studies by PwC, McKinsey and others, who forecast millions of jobs to be lost, or the fact that there is consensus that there will be massive job loss but that estimates very wildly about how many and when.

Experts in the field like AI Investor and scientist Kai Fu Lee openly address the massive job loss and urge serious consideration at a public policy level.

New jobs will be created, but net job creation is not guaranteed; like a Great Recession in job loss but potentially far greater: it is very much about replacing workers.

Request: Feedback, Links, Resources

Q: Most importantly, what do *you* think?
Q: Anything I should add, change, improve?
A: http://tsunami.ai/contact

Additional Resources

www.techemergence.com - good source of news and information about the AI industry

VentureBeat AI Weekly Newsletter
https://venturebeat.com/newsletters/

MIT Technology Review
www.technologyreview.com
> publication, digital access, as well as some things you can subscribe to without necessarily paying.

www.quanta.com - quantum computing

APPENDIX B: TSUNAMI.AI

Please visit http://tsunami.ai for links, additional interviews, and other resources. Your feedback on the book would be greatly appreciated and you can use the contact form on the site. You are also welcome to invite me on LinkedIn at http://linkedin.com/in/tekelsey